Reclaiming My Soul

From

The Lost And Found

By

Lisa J. Whaley

ISBN: 1-4140-7232-5 (e-book)
ISBN: 1-4140-7231-7 (Paperback)
ISBN: 1-4140-7230-9 (Dust Jacket)

Library of Congress Control Number: 2004090869

This book is printed on acid free paper.

Printed in the United States of America
Bloomington, IN

1stBooks - rev. 02/17/04

DEDICATION

For Mom and Dad.

Through your example,
I learned about unconditional love,
the meaning of commitment,
and the power of faith and prayer.
You have been there for me
every step of my journey through life,
and I am so blessed to have
you as parents.

ACKNOWLEDGMENTS

Writing a book is a huge undertaking and a significant challenge. So many people helped me in countless ways, and I dare not attempt to mention them all for fear of inadvertently leaving someone out. I am sincerely grateful to everyone.

However, I would be remiss if I didn't mention a few people who were instrumental in helping me turn my dream into reality. They were there with me every step of the way, offering guidance, advice, candid feedback, and encouragement.

First and foremost, I have to give thanks to God. He picked me up and carried me along the way when I was too weak to stand.

My gifted and talented editor, Amy Meadows of Green Meadows Communications, LLC – thank you for working magic with my words without compromising the integrity of my story.

Terri Hall, Diane Trachtenberg, Carolyn Wallace, Marilyn Johnson, Pam Moye, and Angela Archon – we started out simply as colleagues a few years back, but I instantly knew there was that special connection with each of you. You have become such dear friends to me, and I now understand the meaning of true friendship. Thank you for being there for me throughout my journey, always encouraging me and sharing with me your candor and honesty.

Nancy Griffin – where would I be without our many marathon phone conversations? You are beautiful inside and out. Thank you for keeping me honest. I cherish the bond of our friendship.

The small circle of women who were my test market – Mary Grace Flantzer, Margaret Ashida, Carmen O'Shea, Marie Wieck, and Peggy Henderson – thank you for your insights, your suggestions, and for enduring the first half of this book chapter-by-chapter as I wrote.

Rhea Moore – your kind voicemails always came at the right moments with the perfect words to keep me going at times when I wanted to give up. You have been such a great friend.

Bob Rohr, who graciously read chapter after chapter, offering me a male's perspective. Your sense of humor was just what I needed and was always right on time. Your instant messages never failed to make me laugh. You are one of the most resourceful people I know. Thank you for just being there for me.

Barbara Ellis – when this book was just an idea in my head, you immediately went into action mode, getting me connected with people you thought could help. You truly are one of the awesome women in this world who has been, and continues to be, a great role model for me.

Jylla Foster, president of Crystal Stairs, Inc. – you are amazing! I can never thank you enough for everything you've helped me with. One phone call to you and you immediately believed in me. Without your guidance and encouragement, this book may have very well continued to be an idea in my head.

Monique Goldman – what can I possibly say? You were the single most significant person in my journey to reclaim my soul. With your help, I am finally rid of the façade. I finally have true self-acceptance. I can never thank you enough.

Dr. Mark Ligorski – when I first met you, your brutally candid style shocked me, but it was just what I needed. At first, I tried to pull the wool over your eyes, but I'm so glad you didn't buy it. Thanks for everything you helped me with.

Hattie Bryant, another exceptional woman in this world! I'm so glad we reconnected. You continue to inspire me with all the great work that you're doing, educating small business owners.

Marian Roach and Marcia Jackson – thank you for bringing the Sterling Women's Weekend to me. My weekend experience fundamentally changed my life, and I will never forget the experience.

Ron Roth – thanks so much for sharing your publishing-industry knowledge with me and for being my second pair of eyes. You and Maria are great friends, and I cherish all the good times we've had.

Kerry Ann Johnson – how fast time has flown by. I met you when you were only 16 and you bravely asked me to mentor you. I can't believe you will soon be going to law school. I'm so proud of you. I've learned as much from you as you have learned from me. You've been like a daughter to me, and I will forever cherish the bond we've created.

Reverend Dr. Charles Ferrara – what an incredible man of God you are. Thank you for your spiritual guidance and your constant prayers.

My publisher, 1st Books Library – thank you for this wonderful opportunity to get my story out to the world.

Richard Falco – you are such a creative and masterful photographer. Thank you for your patience and for capturing the exact look I wanted for the cover photo.

Brian Barry –thank you for all of the time and energy you put into cover concept ideas. Your creativity brought to light all the cover possibilities for me.

James Garber – thank you for your masterful cover design and your great flexibility in working with me.

My family – Mom, Dad, Granny, Berthina, Annette, and Lorenzo. Thank you for your unconditional love, your constant support, and your prayers. You never let me stop believing in myself. You have always been there for me.

And last but certainly not least – my loving husband, Jim, and our two beautiful daughters, Kristin and Jennifer. You are my reason for being. I love the three of you so much. You endured this journey with me as I reclaimed my soul. You stuck with me throughout this entire book writing process, listening to chapter after chapter and putting up with my odd and late night writing hours. Thank you for allowing me to share so many intimate, and sometimes painful details about our lives, and for giving up your privacy. I am so grateful that we are all back together again, looking better than ever inside and out.

Finally, thank you to all the readers who have bought and read this book. My hope and prayer is that you have found something in this book that has inspired you and will help you *reclaim* your soul and *keep* it out of the lost and found!

CONTENTS

FORWARD

A Message From Dr. Mark Ligorki

So much of human suffering revolves around the stories we make up about ourselves and our situations and the ones we tell other people. It is not so much that people lie or are deliberately misleading, but they fall into traps and routines, and it becomes easier to accept these stories even though they ring hollow and, in the final analysis, do not serve us well.

In *Reclaiming My Soul From The Lost And Found*, Lisa Whaley takes us down the road of her life and how her struggles and suffering become the motivation to find "the naked truth" behind the lovely façade of a "perfect life" and achieve a deeper and more satisfying experience of life, her family, and her faith. Not content to merely feel better for herself, she has offered us her story as an inspiration and a trail guide to help us find our own way through a world where we can be distracted by superficial and transient success or struggles and forget those principles and beliefs that are the true foundation of a well-lived life.

She shares her story in a candid and unguarded way, unafraid to let us see the difficulties she had to surmount and the mistakes she made along the way. Instead of shame or embarrassment, her return to herself has so reaffirmed her confidence and sense of self that she can talk about her life with enthusiasm, knowing that this book will serve others and help them avoid some of the mistakes she made.

Although the story will first attract women caught up in a world of conflicting priorities, both men and women struggling with multiple demands will enjoy and profit from Lisa Whaley's compelling and enlightening story.

Mark Ligorski, MD
Director, North Court Psychotherapy Center, Danbury, Connecticut
Clinical Assistant Professor of Psychiatry, New York Medical College

PROLOGUE

"Get the fuck out of my room." These were the words spoken by my then 14-year-old daughter on Saturday, September 21, 2002, when I entered her room and woke her up at 5:30 AM accompanied by a rather large male and female from a youth escort service I had hired and flown in from Utah to take her away. They were to escort her to Redcliff Ascent, a Therapeutic Youth Wilderness Program for struggling teens, located in the mountains and desert of Utah. It was what I prayed would be the end of a year and a half of living hell and the beginning of a miraculous healing that would enable both of us to reclaim our souls from the lost and found. In an act of pure desperation and hopelessness, it was the only thing I could do to try to save her life and my own. She had spiraled so far out of control and entered a world of rapid self-destruction. She was drowning in a massive sea of sex, drugs, and alcohol and was taking everyone in our family down with her.

As I stood watching from my bedroom window while they put her in the car, I sobbed with feelings of guilt and despair, but also relief. I could see her face and could tell by her expression that she knew this was the end of life as she had known it. It was as if she had an angelic look of calmness about her, resolving that someone was finally rescuing her from her own nightmare. I knew she had no idea what she was in for or the long and winding road ahead. But the only thing that mattered at that moment was that I knew she was safe. I knew that there would be no more nights of wondering where she was – if she was dead or alive – and having my body tremble with fear every time the phone rang, wondering if this would be the call from the morgue asking me to come identify her body.

In between the salty taste of my own tears and bending over the toilet vomiting, it was as if every detail of my own life flashed through my mind. I couldn't comprehend how we had gotten to this point. Where did I go wrong? How could I, the girl who "had it all," have possibly reached this instant in life? After all, we had been living the American Dream, or so I thought. We had accomplished all the things that others so easily characterize as success – we had "arrived." My husband and I were both executives in our respective companies; we had two beautiful and intelligent daughters, a beautiful home, three luxury cars, three dogs, and even an exotic bird. We were an all around happy family, or so we appeared.

But the dream had become a treacherous nightmare, and I hoped to wake up and find that my world was still perfect. But it was not a dream; it was cold reality slapping me in the face so hard I could barely stand up. I fell on my knees and resorted to the one thing I had learned in my life, if I had learned nothing else. I prayed the most heartfelt prayer and told God if he was trying to get my attention, he had it. I told him that I was leaving everything in his hands, and if I never trusted him before, if I ever doubted his almighty power before, then I asked him to forgive me for I had nowhere else to turn but to him. I was at rock bottom, and no one could save me but him.

INTRODUCTION

From the time I was about 14, the same age my daughter was when I sent her away, I always talked about writing a book someday. For the past 30 years, as I would experience different situations, good and bad, I would log them in the back of my mind as book material – that is, if I could ever get the courage to actually write one. Truthfully, I never thought I really would. After all, I didn't think there was anything profoundly unique or interesting enough about my life that other people would actually want to read. I'm not a famous celebrity or a politician. I'm just like every other woman out there trying to get through life one day at a time.

But after September 21, 2002, I started rethinking the uniqueness of my life. Throughout my life's journey, my mind has been plagued continually with thoughts of sharing my experiences with others, particularly women. These thoughts were now tugging at the core of my soul and had become almost an obsession. I decided that it was no longer acceptable for me to fantasize about what I have always had a passion to do. It was time for me to turn my dream into reality and attempt to help other women perhaps find solace and strength in reading about my experiences, which may not be that different than their own.

I now know unequivocally that I am not the only woman who has hit the sandy bottom of the deep and massive sea. But with the shoreline in sight, I have the freedom and the power to let go of my pride and ego and to document my experiences for you without the pretty coverings. My story has to be told in the nakedness of truth. I hope for any woman out there who's drowning in your own sea of misery that you'll find something in this book that will give you the strength and courage to grab hold of a lifeline and start pulling yourself in. As hopeless as any situation may seem at the moment, I am a witness and can assure you that brighter tomorrows are possible.

Much encouragement to write this book came from other women, friends, and colleagues, who have told me that I am an inspiration to them, that I am great at motivating others, and that I have no idea what a positive effect my high energy, enthusiasm, and zest for life has on others. Little did they know that I actually lost my zest for life. I thought it would be easier to be dead than to continue living and had seriously contemplated suicide.

I sincerely believe that through sharing our own experiences, we grow and become stronger beings. And perhaps, if even just one person will have an "aha moment," an expression often used by Oprah Winfrey, that changes the course and direction of her own life, the sharing is worth it. In the spirit of womanly sisterhood, we owe it to ourselves to help each other to become the best that each of us can be physically, emotionally, and spiritually.

As a wife, a mother, and an IBM executive who everyone perceived as "having it all," I think it is time for me to give something back. All I have to give is myself, my innermost thoughts and feelings and my own personal experiences, which may help someone else as she embarks on her own personal journey. I made the mistake of trying to have it all – all at the same time. I almost lost everything in the process. One day I realized that my soul was somewhere in the lost and found, and I decided I was going to go back and reclaim it. It was a liberating feeling. For the first time in my life I felt like I was making decisions and changes in my life based on what I wanted to do, not based on everyone else's perceptions or expectations of me. In all honestly, much of my life has been a bit of a façade. The structure looked great, but the core was weak and fragile. Over the past few years, a strong wind blew in, and the facade starting tumbling down. It was like "the perfect storm" – the worst thing that ever happened to me and yet the best thing that ever happened to me.

Some of the things in this book may come as a bit of a surprise to my family, friends, and colleagues – people who know me or think that they know me. But that's precisely the point. No one ever really knew the real me because I didn't really even know myself. Maybe at different points in my life I have had glimpses of who I was. But somewhere on my journey through life, I took a wrong detour and became a creation of other people's images of me. I got caught up in that creation, and that's when my soul ended up in the lost and found – to the detriment of my husband and my two daughters. It's a phenomenon that I believe is happening to many women in our fast-paced society today as we juggle the demands of work and family or just life. But I've got my soul back now, reclaimed with a new spirit and a sense of purpose. Although there are times when I still feel like I'm in the ocean treading water, I'm no longer drowning and gasping for air. I've been a great swimmer for most of my life, and I am swimming with everything I've got in me. I know I'm heading for dry land.

While I've never thought of myself as a very religious person, I've always been very spiritual. I have always believed that God has a plan for each of us. Sometimes it is in our weakest hours that we allow God to come into our lives to do his best work. And Lord knows I was in my weakest hour. Often, it is when we are in the depths of despair that we turn to God because we feel there is nowhere else to go. I have learned that it is only then that we finally may submit to or perhaps comprehend how God wants to use us to work his plan for us, through us. So God, if you're listening, and I know you are, please give me the strength and courage to use the precious gifts that you've blessed me with to reach, help, and touch others through the content of this book.

This is my story...

CHAPTER ONE

The Choice of Life or Death

The weather was quite reflective of my mood on this particular autumn day in 2002. The sky was gray and full of clouds with no chance of sunshine in the forecast. For five months, I had been battling a serious blood disorder, but I realized that my physical illness was the least of my problems. It was my emotional state that was killing me.

For the preceding 12 months, it was if everything in my life had been nothing but a downpour of rain. I was caught in "the perfect storm" and felt as if I had nowhere to run for shelter. Still clad in my pajamas, I simply picked up my car keys, walked into my closed garage, sat in my car, and cranked it up. I had decided to choose death over life. I wanted to close my eyes, peacefully fall asleep, and never wake up again.

I had never felt so alone in my entire life. My oldest daughter was in Utah attending Redcliff Ascent's Therapeutic Wilderness Program for struggling teens. My younger daughter was at school. I was supposed to be

1

at work, but I had called my assistant that morning and informed her that I was extremely ill. I told her to cancel all of my meetings and appointments for that day and inform my manager of my absence. My husband, Jim, was in Atlanta, as we had temporarily separated.

He had left two weeks prior, and I felt like he had left me in a pile of shit - literally. The morning he left for Atlanta, our septic tank backed up, and we had raw sewage backing up in the toilets, the bathtubs, and even the washing machine. He simply called a plumber and a septic tank company and left before they arrived.

As I sat in my car with the engine running, two prevailing thoughts entered my mind. I thought of my younger daughter and the fact that she would be the one to come home from school to find me slumped over the steering wheel in the front seat of my car. I couldn't imagine the traumatic effect it would have on her for the rest of her life. My second thought, as sick as it may be, was IBM. I couldn't help but think what all of my colleagues would say about me. My legacy at IBM would be, "The bright and shining star who self destructed. Maybe she didn't have what it takes after all."

I turned the engine off and sat there for about 30 minutes. I couldn't even cry. I was totally numb. I felt as if I had no soul. I knew that I was seriously ill - physically, emotionally, and spiritually. I felt as if I was just some insignificant item that had been tossed into the lost and found waiting for its owner to come back and reclaim it. This was the defining moment for me as I knew that my *soul* was in the lost and found, and I decided I was going back to reclaim it.

I got out of my car, went into the house, and picked up the phone. I then made a call that saved my life. I called IBM's Employee Assistance Program (EAP) hotline. I was quite familiar with the EAP, which is available for employees who need help with everything from mental health issues to substance abuse. I had the number memorized because I had used it often in the preceding months when I was trying to find help for my daughter. That day, I spoke for an hour with a clinician. I told her I had just tried to commit suicide by carbon monoxide poisoning but couldn't go through with it. I poured my heart out to her. I was almost incoherent, rambling in my thoughts and words. I actually don't remember very much about the conversation, but I do recall telling her, "I need help. I've been trying to get an appointment with a psychiatrist for over a week, but no one can see me for at least three weeks. I can't wait that long – I may be dead by then."

I have to admit that I don't remember the clinician's name, but she was wonderful – a true godsend. She mostly listened, but every once in a while she must have said something appropriate because I recall small feelings of hope. She asked me if I wanted an ambulance to come get me and take me to the hospital. I assured her that I had made the choice to live and that I was not going to try to harm myself again. She stayed on the phone with me and used her other line to try to set up an appointment with a psychiatrist for me right away. She was able to get an appointment for me for 4:00 PM that afternoon. It was about 11:00 AM when we finished our call, and she called me back every 30 minutes to check on me and see how I was doing.

I was so weak physically and emotionally that I could barely manage the strength to take a shower and get dressed. The most mundane and ordinary tasks felt monumental to me, but I was driven by the thought that all of my life I had been perceived as this "strong and determined woman" who would let nothing bring her down.

I watched the clock tick minute by minute for four and a half hours. As I waited for the time to come for me to leave for my appointment, I began thinking about my life. I reached deep into the memory bank of my childhood. I remembered that I had been raised with a very solid foundation based on love, understanding, great values and principles, and a strong sense of spirituality and faith. I was not raised to be a coward or to give up. I was raised believing that I could do anything I put my mind to and that no obstacles where so insurmountable that they couldn't be overcome.

I finally left for my appointment. During the 20-minute drive, I was almost fixated on the beauty of the fall leaves changing colors and floating to the ground. It was somewhat symbolic – I too was shedding my leaves. I knew it was the beginning of the healing process for me. I was finally reaching out for help. I realized that I had broken many of my own principles regarding keeping harmony between life and work. There was nothing harmonious in my life or work at the moment. I was singing way off key and very much out of tune. My mind, body, and soul had completely shut down. But I knew with time, they would be back in sync. I was determined that I would do whatever work was necessary and ahead of me to ensure that it happened. I was ready to grow new leaves.

I started out that gloomy autumn day making a choice of death. But by the end of the day, I had decided to choose life. I knew I was on my way to join the land of the living again. It was a significant decision, and I get cold chills every time I think about it now. If I had followed through on the other choice, I would never have seen all the bright days that I have lived to see. I couldn't fathom then that there would be sunshine once again in my life. Even though it still continues to pour rain some days, I just imagine that I'm "Annie" in the Broadway musical singing "The sun will come out tomorrow." And it always does.

I now comprehend that one usually does not get to the spot I found myself in that dreary morning overnight. It's a slow process that evolves

4

over time. So, I want to start at the beginning and share with you the events that created the person I thought I was, led to the awareness of the person I found I wasn't, and triggered the self-discovery of the person I now know that I am.

CHAPTER TWO

A Solid Foundation

On April 4, 1960, I entered this vast and complex world. While my given name was Oleatha Adrine Jones, everyone always called me Lisa. My mother made the decision to legally change my name when I entered first grade so there would not be any confusion in my school records. I was so glad because I never liked the name Oleatha. I was born and raised in Miami, Florida, and consider myself to be blessed, having grown up in a close-knit family with loving parents, two older sisters, and an older brother. My maternal grandmother, Granny, lived with us as well. She is still living with my mother today and is as spunky as ever at age 89.

My parents, Burk and Josie Jones, constantly told all of us that we could do whatever we wanted to do in life and that nobody could stop us, except for ourselves. They were great believers in Martin Luther King, Jr.'s mantra that one shouldn't be "judged by the color of their skin but by the content of their character." They strived every day to expose us to a diverse perspective on life – racially, culturally, and socio economically. They both worked hard and earned a good living to afford us the things they didn't have growing up. While we weren't rich, I grew up thinking we were, for I had everything I needed and, for the most part, just about everything I ever wanted. As a child, other kids called me "rich girl." When I would ask my mom if we were rich, she always would respond, "Yes, we are rich with love." It's a statement I found myself using with my own kids when they asked that very same question many years later.

Don't get me wrong; we weren't the Waltons by any stretch of the imagination. We had our fair share of family conflicts and problems. But what distinctly stands out in my memories of my childhood is that I sincerely can say it was a very happy one. I remember that we spent a lot of time together, and there was a lot of laughter and a lot of love. We were a touchy-feely family, and we told each other "I love you" often.

My family was very active in the Second Baptist Church, attending Sunday school, church, bible study, and youth activities. Although my faith was shaken later in my life and I questioned my religious beliefs for a long time, church undoubtedly was a big part of my childhood. My family would sing spirituals and church hymns together often at home and in the car on our many road trip vacations. We always had a piano, and while all of us took piano lessons, I'm the only one who stuck with it. I fondly remember my mom sitting at the piano plucking out a tune with us all gathered around singing. We all had pretty decent voices and could harmonize quite well. But it was my second oldest sister, Berthina, who could really, as they would say, "sang." If there would have been an *American Idol* back then, she could have definitely been a contender.

We had a beautiful home that was very comfortable and large by other people's standards for that period of time. It was an open, airy, and spacious ranch-style house with five bedrooms, three bathrooms, and a large yard. I remember always being very proud to bring people to our house. It was always very warm and inviting, as well as very neat and orderly. My mom was almost obsessed with things being clean and tidy, which is a trait that was passed down to me. I can be rather anal about things being organized and in their proper place – something that drives my husband and kids crazy.

There was always an abundance to eat as Granny did almost all of the cooking, and she could really "throw down," as folks would say. I remember our home being a little like Grand Central Station. We always had lots of people coming and going. Our house was sort of the hangout. All of our friends enjoyed spending time in our home because they considered my parents to be cool – easy to talk to and nonjudgmental. Sometimes it was as if our friends seemed to enjoy our parents' company more than ours.

While my parents were very strict with my older sisters and brother, they were very liberal with me. There is a six-year age difference between my brother and me, and by the time I reached adolescence, they had already experienced the trials and tribulations of raising teenagers. They had learned what worked and what didn't with my siblings and took a slightly different approach with me. I was allowed do things, such as date, at a much earlier age than my siblings. I had a lot more freedom. My siblings still remind me to this day that I had it much easier than they did. In many ways, I spent most of my adolescence much like an only child. My siblings were all out of the house attending college. I was somewhat spoiled in terms of getting just about anything I asked for, but I was not rotten.

Nevertheless, I was definitely a daddy's girl and could get pretty much anything I wanted out of him. My father was always a very quiet, mild-mannered man, but when he got mad he could give you a look that would make the hairs on the back of your neck stand up. My father never smoked or drank. I can probably count on 10 fingers the number of times I can even recall him cursing. He taught me to drive when I was only 12 years old, much before I was of legal age to be behind the wheel. But no matter how old I was, I always knew that he was a good provider. When I was quite young, my father worked three jobs simultaneously – teaching high school, drawing architectural plans for house and building renovations, and working at a department store on weekends. He wanted to ensure that his family could have the best of everything.

Sadly, my father had glaucoma and always knew that he was going to go blind slowly, which he eventually did. Losing his sight was heartbreaking for me because I recognized the great passion he had for doing architectural work, something you definitely need your eyesight to do. At the beginning of 2000, my father became quite ill, having had several strokes. In February of 2002, our family jointly made the tough decision to place him in a nursing home. He could no longer see or walk, and he could barely talk. He couldn't swallow, so a feeding tube had to be placed in his stomach so he could eat. Seeing my father in this stage of his life has been a tremendous emotional struggle for me to deal with. Although my father has handled his illness with great humility, I can only imagine the sadness he must feel.

I always had a good relationship with my mom, although we clashed a lot and still do at times. Perhaps it's because we are Aries, which makes us very strong-willed individuals and natural born leaders. Throughout my childhood, my mom was like the rock in our family. She has always been

9

an extremely strong woman who lets nothing get her down. She grew up very poor and, at 17, married my father, who was in his first year of teaching at the high school she attended and also ten years her senior. My mom felt that getting married, even at such a young age, was her ticket out of poverty. She had spent her own childhood raising her four younger brothers and a younger sister, and she was ready to relinquish that responsibility. She knew that she would have a good life with my father.

Many people may have thought that my mom wore the pants in our family, but nothing could be further from the truth. My dad, indisputably, was the one in control – he just let my mom think she was. And as quiet and mild mannered as my father was, my mom had no problem being heard. She too could give those looks that not only made the hairs on your neck stand up, but also made them feel like they were on fire. Yet, my mom has always had a big heart and has proven herself to be a very caring and giving person. She has taken people into our home and given them a place to stay when they had nowhere else to go.

As strong as she was, my mom did have one particular vulnerability that stands out in my mind – smoking. I will never forget the day she quit. When I was about six years old, my mom got very sick one day. The image of her in the bathroom standing over the toilet praying to God that if he healed her she would never pick up a cigarette again is etched in my mind as if it were yesterday. There was something very powerful about seeing my mom in such a submissive state praying to God. She took her cigarettes, and broke them in half, and flushed them down the toilet. She has never touched another cigarette since then.

My mom has always been a praying woman. She prays about everything. "Just turn it over to the Lord" is a phrase I grew up hearing constantly and have heard throughout my lifetime whenever I've had any type of problem. Growing up, I was a little afraid of my mom because she always seemed to know things that I would have preferred she didn't. I always believed she had some psychic abilities, which made me feel like I could never tell her a lie and get away with it. To this very day, even though we live miles apart in different parts of the country, my mom will call me when she senses something is wrong, And she is always right on the money. My mom and I remain very close, and it would be highly unusual for us to go as much as a week without talking on the phone. In fact, to this day, even though I'm married with my own family and have traveled all over the world, my mom still expects me to let her know when I'm traveling and where I'm going and to call to let her know that I've arrived safely. When I go back to Miami to visit, she still reminds me to lock my car doors. I guess no matter how grown up I think I am or how successful I appear, I will always be her baby girl. She used to tell me, "Some day you'll have kids of your own, and then you'll understand that a good mother never stops worrying about her children." I never knew how right she'd be.

Having my Granny live with us was great. She and I were like two peas in a pod when I was young. Before I was old enough to fix my own hair, Granny used to do it for me. She would brush it, slick it down, and put it in two braids. I always had long, wavy, curly hair, "good hair" as people would call it. I always hated my hair because it was high-maintenance and hard to take care of. But Granny didn't mind it at all. She also loved to sew and used to make many of my clothes. When I was in junior high school, micro-mini dresses with the matching underpants – I think they were called sizzlers – were in style. Granny made one for me in every conceivable color and fabric.

11

She had her own room and bathroom in our house, and I always wanted to sleep in her room with her. For many years, I actually slept in the bed with her because it was where I always felt safe. She would tell me stories, and we would lie in bed laughing and talking like two old souls, about life, boys, and even God. She and my grandfather were divorced, and I would ask her things about him because I didn't know him very well. But she never wanted to talk about him, leading me to believe that he caused a lot of pain in her life. Sometimes I think my mom was a little jealous of the bond I had with Granny because I always thought she was so wise. I thought Granny knew everything and could do anything. She could do no wrong in my eyes.

While my sisters and brother and I are all fairly close, we sort of divided ourselves in terms of our relationships with each other. I always called my oldest sister and my brother by their middle names, Annette and Lorenzo. I have no idea why; their first names are Debra and Burk. Annette and Lorenzo were the wild ones in our family, while my other sister, Berthina, and I had more of a bond. If there was trouble to be found, Annette and Lorenzo would find it. Perhaps Berthina and I were just a little smarter in the way we went about doing things – whether they were good or bad – so we rarely got ourselves in trouble.

Annette was tall, thin, and beautiful. I didn't really get to know her or get close to her until I became an adult. Maybe it was because of the 12-year age difference between us. But I remember her being extraordinarily funny; she could always make me laugh and still can. It wasn't what she would say, but it was how she would say it. She would make funny faces and change her voice, which never failed to make me to go into hysterics. Yet, there was one situation that didn't leave me doubled over from

12

laughing and actually caused Annette to feel bad for many years because she was responsible for a very bad scar on my right ankle. While I have no recollection of the incident that put the scar there, I've been told the story many times. I was four years old, and she was riding her bicycle with me on the back. My ankle got caught in the spokes and, even though I was screaming and crying for her to stop, she didn't realize what was happening and kept peddling. The spokes tore into the flesh of my ankle and went down to the bone, leaving me with forty stitches and a lifetime scar.

In my adult life, Annette and I have grown much closer over the years. She has so much patience and always tries to see the bright side of everything. She can quote scriptures from the Bible that apply to any life situation, and her positive outlook on life has become a source of inspiration to me.

My brother, Lorenzo, and I never really got along. I've sometimes wondered if it was because I replaced him as the baby of the family when he was six years old. He used to be really mean to me and teased me a lot. He used to call me "Mexican girl" and would tell me that our parents found me on the doorsteps of our house. I have to admit, I did do things to irritate him, and I was a bit of a tattletale. I would tell my parents when he had girls over when they weren't home. He would bribe me not to tell. I would take the bribe, but then I would always somehow slip up and tell anyway.

My brother has always been somewhat of a ladies man – they love him, and he loves them. When I was younger, I used to wonder what it was that women saw in my brother, since they always seemed to practically flock at his feet. As I got older, I understood - as Lorenzo has a big heart and a way of making people feel special. He has a gift for working with special-needs children and adults. He seems to be able to reach them and get them to do things that other people can't. He has worked at several group homes where kids are placed when they're waiting to be adopted or waiting for a foster home. He and his wife have even been foster parents for kids who've been removed from their own homes because of abuse. He seems to love what he does, and he's great at it.

My second oldest sister, Berthina, and I have always been very close. We're very different yet quite similar. She was always the brain in the family, and, as I mentioned, she has a beautiful voice. She was my idol growing up, and I always wanted to do everything she did. When she was in high school, she won a Silver Knight, an award sponsored by the *Miami Herald*, which was a very big deal and a considerable honor. Berthina won for her outstanding achievement in Social Sciences. During my high school years, I too was nominated for a Silver Knight, but I didn't win. It was one of the earliest major disappointments in my life.

Growing up, Berthina always had a book in hand. I think in many ways she grew up feeling a little insecure in terms of her physical appearance. She was a little chubby, had short, kinky hair, and wore glasses. But she had the kind of inner beauty that people were always drawn to. Even with her intelligence and many achievements throughout her life, I think it took her many years to become self-confident and comfortable in her own skin. When I was in junior high, I went to spend a few days with her at her college, Fisk University. I will always remember that trip because it gave me a first-hand look at what college life would be like. We had a great time, and she seemed so proud to show off her baby sister to everyone and to brag about how smart I was.

Berthina was always very protective of me and has been there for me through thick and thin. I don't think I could have endured without her when I was at the lowest point in my life. She has been one of the greatest sources of strength for me, as she is the epitome of a survivor. She lived through her first husband's suicide at the age of 24 - a tragic event that affected me more than anyone could have known. I looked up to Bobby, and for years I could not understand how someone could reach the point where he would be willing to take his own life. I didn't understand until I found myself in the same situation many years later.

Even after this tragic loss, my sister found love again with George, one of her closest friends, and married for a second time. During their second pregnancy, amniocentesis revealed that her child would have Down syndrome. While others may have chosen to abort the pregnancy, Berthina and George never considered the option. They let their baby girl, Jessica, come into the world and experience life just as she was. Through Berthina's example, I have learned that you must deal with whatever life throws in your direction. You can never give up because tomorrow may be a better day. And when I personally questioned whether or not I would have the strength to go on in my life, Berthina was there to help me see another tomorrow.

Unfortunately, my paternal grandparents died before I was born, so I never knew them. While I had many aunts and uncles who played important roles in my young life, there's one relative that affected my life significantly. She was my father's only sibling, Auntie, as we used to call her. She lived a few blocks away from us and was married to an alcoholic, Uncle Farley. When I was about 11 years old and went to spend the night at their house, Uncle Farley tried to kiss me and put his tongue in my mouth. It made me feel so dirty and disgusting. His breath stunk and reeked of alcohol. It's probably the reason why I feel sick to my stomach even today when someone's breath smells like alcohol. I ran out of the room and told my Auntie that I wanted to go home. I was crying, and she kept asking me

15

why I wanted to go home. I didn't tell her what happened because I didn't want her to feel hurt, and I didn't think she would believe me. She finally agreed to take me home, and I think she sensed something had happened when I was in the room alone with my uncle. It was years later before I ever told anyone about that incident. It never happened again, but I never wanted to go visit them after that.

Actually, I don't think Auntie ever really liked me very much. She was always fairly polite to me, but she definitely treated me differently than my other siblings. I do remember her letting me light her cigarettes when I was quite young. I often wonder if that's why I started smoking, a bad habit that I've struggled with giving up for years. Auntie died in 1989, and I didn't attend her funeral.

My mom always would say, "The family that prays together stays together." And we prayed all the time. Perhaps that's why, as a child, I developed a warped view on life that nothing bad would ever happen to me. Even when I mistakenly was convinced that the KKK was banging on the door of a relative I was visiting, I wasn't the least bit afraid. While so many people start out in life with a shaky foundation, I consider myself blessed, as that was not the case with me. I had a solid foundation from the start, being part of a family where I felt unconditionally loved. I believe this strong foundation has had a great impact on who I've become and who I will always be.

I thought that my husband and I had laid a strong foundation for our own family, but I would later learn that our foundation was built on sinking soil. It would take a long time for us to realize it. When we did, it was almost too late.

CHAPTER THREE

School Days

Like most children, I learned a great deal about the world and myself when I was in school. At a very young age, I was introduced to a variety of issues, never really understanding what they meant and how they would affect me later in life. From how people perceive differences between boys and girls to the pressure to fit into just the right group of friends, my experiences helped formulate principles and standards that I adhere to today. Yet, those school days, which fundamentally were quite happy, also produced something else – my innate desire and life long quest to satisfy others, and not necessarily myself.

My elementary school years were filled with all the innocence that childhoods should be made of. I attended Whispering Pines Elementary School, which was not the school in our school district. In fact, it was quite a distance from our house, but my parents selected it for me to attend because they thought that I would get a better education. It was a brand new school, and I was the first and only black child in attendance from first through sixth grade. For much of my time at Whispering Pines, a taxicab driver that my parents paid transported me to and from school. The school librarian was a friend of our family who lived not far from us, and sometimes I would ride with her. I never felt any different from any other kid at the school. To be honest, I didn't even look that different. It was Miami, and everyone had that pecan-colored tan complexion. Being of light skin and having long hair, I didn't stand out significantly from anyone else. But all the kids at Whispering Pines quickly realized that I was a "colored" girl - the nomenclature for blacks back then. However, it never really seemed to matter to them, and it never mattered to me that I wasn't one of "them."

Most of my friends were Jewish, and my two best friends at school were Robin and Leslie. I spent many nights at sleepovers in both of their homes, and their families always made me feel welcome. Sometimes their parents allowed me to sleep over on weeknights since I lived so far away. Leslie's family had a pool and a beautiful boat, which I went out on several times. I think that's when my love of the water and the ocean began, even though I wasn't a very good swimmer back then. On one occasion, I remember being in Leslie's pool and ending up in the deep end, panicking and starting to drown. Leslie quickly came to my rescue, and I practically drowned her trying to save myself. When we both got to the side of the pool, she was laughing hysterically thinking that I was just playing around. She never knew that I was really drowning, and I never told her any differently, for even back then I had a big ego and a lot of pride. But I vowed to myself then and there that I would become a great swimmer. And I did.

We didn't have to wear uniforms at Whispering Pines, but girls couldn't wear pants. We had to wear dresses or skirts. When I was in third grade, we had a substitute teacher one day, and she wouldn't allow the girls to play on the monkey bars at recess. I thought this was grossly unfair that the boys could but the girls couldn't, early evidence that I believed that women and men should be treated equally. I don't know what got into me, but, on a whim, I ran over and climbed up on the monkey bars and hung upside down. There I was with my skirt and shirt flipped over my head flashing the world with my pretty - and hopefully clean - white panties showing! The teacher raced over and yanked me off the bars and made me sit in time out.

As I sat in the grass fuming, a girl from another class whom I didn't know came over and sat next to me. She said, "I know your name. You're Lisa." I didn't respond. She then said, "Even though you're colored and I'm Jewish, we're just the same." I still didn't respond, as I was still seething over lack of equality between boys and girls relative to the monkey-bar incident. She then took a safety pin from her skirt and told me to hold out my finger. I tentatively held out my finger, and she pricked me. Then she pricked herself and said, "See, both of our blood is red. We're just the same." I looked at her rather perplexed, thinking that this girl was weird. Blood was dripping down my finger, and I promptly asked her to go get me a Band-Aid. I didn't know then what an impact that pricking incident would have on my life in terms of "sameness" until years later.

I was really happy on the rare occasions when my mom could drive me to school because I was sort of embarrassed about showing up in a taxi. On one of these rare occasions, I became suspicious that my mom had some psychic abilities. My mom and I were in the car, and a car passed us. The man was driving a little erratically, weaving in and out of traffic. My mother said, "That fool is going to hit us. Put on your seatbelt." This was before seatbelts were mandatory. I distinctly remember wondering how could he hit us when he was two cars ahead of us, albeit in the next lane over. No more than two minutes later, there was a big bang and a big jolt of our car. Low and behold, the fool had hit us from behind. His lane must have stopped moving, and he weaved in behind us and hit us really hard. Fortunately, we weren't hurt, but it scared the hell out of me – not that we were hit, but that my mom somehow knew we were going to get hit. And while this episode made me ponder my mother's extrasensory abilities, I became convinced of her gift through even more incidents over the course of my life.

Some of my fondest memories about my elementary school days were playing in my neighborhood. There were lots of kids, and we used to play every kind of ball we could think of in the street. We were fortunate to live in a neighborhood with several streets that rarely had any traffic. It was very safe, and we always had fun. My next-door neighbor, who also happened to be my only real boyfriend from first through twelfth grade, was Herb. We called him Herbie back then. He and his younger brother, Jeff, and I used to play *Mod Squad*, a popular detective show on TV back then. Herb would be Pete, Jeff was Link, and I was Julie. Of course, on the show, it was obvious that Pete and Julie liked each other. He was always comforting and protecting her. They were always hugging and holding hands. Herb and I made sure we took full advantage of that in our role-playing. We also played Batman and Robin, and I was always Batgirl. I never wanted to be Catwoman because she was evil, and I never liked cats anyway!

Before I started to grow breasts, I thought I was like one of the boys. I would run around with Herb and Jeff in their front yard and be just as rough as they were. During those hot, sticky Miami summer days, they would take their shirts off, and I would too! I could play football just as well as any of the boys in our neighborhood. I always wanted to play the quarterback, probably an early indication that I would always want to be the one calling the shots – the one in control. Even though I had chronic asthma, which I outgrew by junior high school, I never let it stop me from doing anything. Of course, it was very convenient that Herb and Jeff's father was a doctor. He used to come over to our house on many occasions to give me a shot when I had a bad attack.

Outside of the kids in my neighborhood, other kids, particularly girls in our surrounding community, didn't like me very much. They often called me names like "half-breed" and "Oreo." They would tell me that I thought I was too cute or too good for them since I went to a "white" school. I would act like their comments didn't bother me, but they really hurt my feelings. One day, I met a girl named Nerissa who was very nice to me. We were both in about the fourth grade at the time. She and I became best friends; in fact, we became lifetime friends, even though the nature of our relationship has changed somewhat over the years.

We complemented each other perfectly. Nerissa was always very petite and had a quiet way about her as a child. I, on the other hand, was rather loud. She too played the piano, and we discovered we were taking piano lessons at the same place. While I was the youngest of four children, she

21

was the oldest of four. As tomboyish as I was, she was always very "girlie." We used to share our darkest, deepest secrets with each other and vowed never to tell. Some of my most memorable times of childhood, adolescence, and even young adulthood involved things that Nerissa and I experienced together. We used to talk about someday writing a tell-all book together.

When it was time for me to move on to junior high school, I begged my parents to let me attend the school in our district, Richmond Heights Junior High. I wanted to go to the same school as all of the other kids in my community. I was tired of living so far away from all of my school friends. My parents agreed, and I was looking forward to the change. My dad was a guidance counselor at RHJH, but I didn't want anyone to know he was my father because I didn't want the other kids to think that I was getting special treatment because of him. Sooner or later, everyone knew anyway. It really wasn't as big of a deal as I thought it would be.

Like most kids, my junior high school years were a critical time in my young life. Being right in the midst of adolescence, puberty, and the struggle to claim my independence, I often felt caught between wanting to still be a little girl and wanting to be all grown up. To my surprise, it only took me a short time to adjust to my new school and new environment. For a while, I didn't exactly know where I fit in at RHJH. The school was integrated and quite diverse, as this was the early- to mid-'70s and the middle of the influx of Cubans to Miami. I had just come from a school environment where I was the only black child, so I never felt caught between having to fit into a group based on race. Everyone at Whispering Pines just accepted me. But at RHJH, especially in my first year there, I often felt like I was being forced into a box and had to choose which group I was going to be a part of. Many of the Spanish kids thought I was Spanish and shunned me somewhat because I didn't speak the language. They thought I was disavowing my heritage. I don't think the white kids knew quite what to make of me. It probably didn't help any that I was in my Pocahontas phase – I wore my hair in two braids over my ears with a headband around my forehead, looking very much like an American Indian, which earned me the nickname Pocahontas for a while.

I was in the band at RHJH and played clarinet. Being in band helped me find my place at RHJH without having to choose a group based on race. As band members, we were a unique clique within ourselves. Nerissa and another friend from my neighborhood, Michael, also were in the band. She played percussion, and he played saxophone. I became good friends with another girl, Shunda, who also played the clarinet. By eighth grade I was very immersed in a clique of girls that included Nerissa, Shunda, and Regina. We had established ourselves as leaders in the school by becoming very involved in the student council and other extracurricular activities. We even formed a singing group, The Pastels, and performed at many school functions. We did just about everything together and always protected each other. We were all good students and made good grades. I continued my trend of being a straight A student. School was easy for me, and I really didn't have to put in much effort to get A's.

As much as I enjoyed hanging out with my girlfriends, I sometimes had a conflict because of the Herbie factor. By this time, we were quite an item and very much in innocent love. I wanted to spend every free minute of the day with him. People always commented about what a cute couple we made. We looked similar and could have passed for brother and sister, although Herb actually had two younger brothers and no sisters. Growing up, I always felt like I was the daughter his parents never had. I was always very close to them, and I still am. When their father was in private practice,

23

he would sometimes take Herb, Jeff, and me with him to the hospital as he made his patient rounds. People would always comment what cute sons and daughter he had. He never corrected them to let them know I was not his daughter.

It's not as if Herb and I couldn't see as much as we wanted of each other; after all, we were next-door neighbors. We even had a pair of walkie-talkies that we shared so we could talk at night while looking at each other through the windows! We were voted "Couple of the Year" in ninth grade. Herb and I thought that we would grow up and get married, and many other people believed that too. It was his youngest brother, Howard, however, who called the most accurate play. Sitting on my front porch one day, I asked Howard if he thought Herb and I would get married. I was very disappointed in his answer and remember it almost verbatim; he said, "No. If you and Herbie go off to different colleges, you'll meet different people and go your separate ways." Howard was no more than about ten years old then, but he called it just as it ended up happening.

I attended Miami Killian Senior High School, and my high school years were an absolute blast. I tried out for the majorette squad my first year at Killian and made it. Being a majorette was a big deal, making you instantly popular. Everyone knew the majorettes. It was every guy's goal to make it with a majorette and every girl's goal to beat one up! We were the clique of all cliques. During high school, I was also a cheerleader for the Miami Dolphins; we were called Dolphin Dolls. This was right before the era when professional football teams started to use older, sexy, and scantily clad girls as cheerleaders or dancers. To be a Dolphin Doll, you had to know how to twirl a baton, do drill team, dance, cheer, and do gymnastics. Making the team was based on talent and not looks. Activities revolving around majorettes and Dolphin Dolls consumed my high school days. We had practice during the week and on weekends, and then, of course, there were the football games, parades, special appearances, and performances. I barely had time to breathe during high school. But I kept my grades up and made mostly A's, graduating in the top four percent in a senior class of 947.

During my senior year of high school, the University of Miami was in need of some additional majorettes on its squad. The university allowed high school majorettes to try out. I made the squad and was thrilled to be able to perform with a college squad while still in high school. Life was good. What more could a girl want? I was 17 and cheering for a professional football team, performing with a college majorette squad, and was an excellent student. I also had the guy every other girl wanted. Herb and I were still an item and by then in real love. However, we went through multiple breakups and make-ups. During our breakups, I would casually go out with other guys, but nobody else could ever seem to hold my attention or capture my heart. Most of those other guys just wanted to try to get into my pants. But Herb was a real gentleman. Not to say that his hormones, like most guys by this age, weren't raging too! But above all, he was a true friend, who genuinely cared about me as a person and always made me feel like a princess.

Looking back on my school years, it's now apparent to me that I was a somewhat stressed-out child. My parents had me in every conceivable activity. There were the multitudes of lessons – piano, guitar, gymnastics, ballet, jazz, tap, swimming, and baton. Then there were all the church activities, social activities, school activities, various pageants, and contests. I took modeling and acting lessons and did some modeling print work; I also had bit parts in two movies. I was involved in sports such as volleyball, basketball and softball. If my parents' goal was to ensure that I became a very well-rounded individual, they succeeded. However, my one regret is that, while I learned to do a lot of things fairly well, I never felt as if I developed any true expertise at any one thing. I didn't feel as if I excelled at anything. Interesting enough, this feeling followed me into my adult life and profession, even though I've enjoyed a successful 22-year career with IBM.

I loved ballet and jazz and often dreamed of being a ballet dancer, but I knew I wasn't good enough. I had trouble spotting, a critical skill for a dancer that allows you to spin around without getting dizzy. Still, in everything I did, I always emerged as the leader. I never had any problem taking control of any situation. Even back then, I had a knack for getting other people to follow my lead. I could get people to do just about anything I wanted them to do. I loved to play the role of psychologist and listen to everyone else's problems and give advice. I had already developed the persona that my life was perfect, that I had it all. Everyone thought I had the total package with all the goods – looks, smarts, and talent. But as I reflect back, I now realize that I did develop expertise in something – living a facade. I enjoyed the attention that I created for myself. I was proud that I could meet and usually exceed everyone else's expectations of me. I never wanted to do anything that I thought would disappoint my parents, or anyone else for that matter. I became great at just going with the flow of life and could always turn on the charm and flash a smile that could make a lion's heart melt. Anytime I was hurting inside, no one knew. It was if I had already become a magnificent master of disguise.

Looking back, I was a pretty good kid. In fact, in my small circle of friends, we were all good kids. While the pressures of society weren't nearly as pronounced as they are today, they were definitely present. Drugs were very much on the scene back then but were never a part of our little world. We had acquaintances who used drugs, but we didn't judge them and they respected us and the fact that drugs weren't our thing. Even drinking alcohol was something that never really appealed to most of us. We weren't little sweet angels, though. We did occasionally sneak off and do things that we shouldn't have done. Occasionally, we would go somewhere different than where we said we were going. And I must admit, I did skip school – but only once! In the grand scheme of things, these were minor transgressions. Perhaps it's because we all grew up with the fear of God in us. If we did anything that we knew was wrong, we were praying hard on Sunday mornings in church asking God for forgiveness. It was drilled into our heads during Sunday school that God would always forgive us if we prayed and asked him to. I took that at face value, and there were a few times I prayed exceptionally hard, even though I had become confused about religion and questioned often exactly what it was I believed in.

This religious confusion was brought about by a youth minister who I really looked up to and had a great deal of admiration for. That is, until I found out from a friend that he was trying to become intimate with her. This was a married man and supposedly a man of God. How hypocritical of him to preach God's word to the youth and try to save our souls while trying to get in a few young girls' pants all at the same time. It really turned me off and made me feel like religion was just a big crock. Every time I set foot in the church and he was there, my stomach would be in knots because I knew what he was really all about. And he knew that I knew. That was a tremendous burden to carry around as a young teen. As the years passed, I finally came to terms with my religious or, more important, my spiritual beliefs. By the time I was 30, I had witnessed so many miracles in my life that I could no longer have any doubt that there was a God. I had come to understand that we are all only human – even religious leaders – and we all make mistakes. God is a forgiving God. It is not for me to judge anyone, as we are each accountable to God and only God. I've been re-convinced of this most recently, since my faith has been tested like never before.

I regret that my husband and I didn't raise our own kids with a strong religious or spiritual foundation. While we went to church, it was sporadic. We never really became very active in a church family. Our kids grew up with little sense of spirituality. Unlike me, they didn't grow up with the fear of God in them. Praying was something they thought you did on the rare occasions when you attended church. I often wonder if my oldest daughter would have made some of the poor choices she did if she had more spirituality. While I have no way of knowing, it's a question that has haunted me.

CHAPTER FOUR

Behind the Gates of Hampton Institute

Upon finishing high school, I had my choice of colleges to attend and could have gone to any Ivy League University. But I had already made up my mind that I wanted to attend a small, private, predominantly black college. I felt like I was having a little bit of an identity crisis relative to my race. I don't know if it had something to do with my first six years of school being in an all white environment, but I always felt more comfortable with white people. Deep inside I never felt like I was black enough and had this desire to come to terms with my blackness.

I selected Hampton Institute, now called Hampton University, as my first choice. Located in Hampton, Virginia, Hampton had an excellent reputation and a beautiful campus on the waterfront. I applied and was accepted. Kathy, another majorette who was a year ahead of me at Miami Killian and also a Dolphin Doll, also attended Hampton. Quite by coincidence, Nerissa applied to Hampton and was accepted as well. We did not plan to go to the same college; it just happened that way. We were both so excited to get into Hampton and to know that we would still be together. We decided to be roommates, which sounded like a good idea at the time, but, in retrospect, it almost ruined our friendship.

Hampton was culture shock to me. It felt a little weird to me to be in an almost totally black environment. But I adjusted and fell in love with Hampton in less than 30 days. My mother flew with me to Hampton to ensure that I got settled with no problems. We arrived on campus in our rental car with a big trunk full of all my belongings. There were a few guys hanging around, and my mom asked them if they would help bring my trunk up to my dorm. They did, and she gave them some money to thank them and told them to look out for me. They said they would, and two of them, Tommy and John, became two of my best friends and were a part of my life during my entire time at Hampton. They always reminded me that they committed to my mom to look after me, and they lived up to that commitment. Ironically, they are both deceased now. Tommy died in 1994 after a serious illness, and John passed away suddenly a few years ago. I was very shocked and saddened by both of their deaths and still think of both of them often with fond memories.

Nerissa and I stayed in Kennedy Hall, an all-girls dorm, our freshman year. Kennedy had a long time reputation of housing beautiful women nicknamed "Kennedy Kittens." We had a very large room, the largest one in the dorm. We met Marian, Marcia, and Beryl (called Sena back then), three other "Kennedy Kittens" with whom we had an instant connection. All three were very attractive. Marian was tall, slender, and extremely fair-skinned with light eyes and hair. I thought at first that she was white. Marcia had the most beautiful smile and always reminded me of a black

30

version of Meg Ryan. Beryl was a complete fascination to me. She had a New York accent, and I loved to listen to the way she talked. She had a laugh like I had never heard before. We had all grown up with similar backgrounds, and, while we were all very different, we all understood each other. We became very good friends and have maintained our friendship on different levels over the years.

I was a business management major with a minor in marketing. My freshman classes were all interesting to me and fairly easy. Nerissa and I both tried out for the majorette squad and were the only freshmen to make it. We became instantly popular and were known as the "Florida Girls." People seemed to be fascinated with the fact that we grew up in Miami - they seem to have this belief that if you grow up in Miami, you live on the beach, which was not the case with either of us. Nerissa quickly gained a reputation for being a very fashionable dresser. She always had beautiful clothes and looked perfectly put together. I wasn't very good at putting outfits together in those days, so I depended on her a lot in that department and learned a lot about fashion. I was very much a jeans and T-shirt kind of girl back then. By college, our relationship had become somewhat competitive in a friendly way. But I always felt like I had to take care of Nerissa – in a nurturing way.

Herb had applied and was accepted to Florida State University. We had broken up at the end of our senior year of high school but were still very good friends and attended the senior prom together. We both left for college with open minds and vowed to always be the best of friends no matter what. While we were still in love, we both knew that a long-distance relationship

31

would be hard. We knew that we would always have a special relationship and that we would always be there for each other. We have continued to live up to that promise and are still great friends to this day.

On my first day at Hampton after Nerissa and I had gotten settled in our room, we went out to walk along the waterfront. It was absolutely breathtaking, and I couldn't believe that I was really there. A car passed by with an incredibly good-looking guy driving it. I said to Nerissa, "Did you see that guy? That's going to be my project." I never in a million years really envisioned what would later come to pass. That evening, we attended a freshman meet-and-greet dance. I was standing around and right before my very eyes was my project. I couldn't believe it. I couldn't help but stare at him and was quite obvious about it. I remember thinking, *please ask me to dance you beautiful specimen of a man.* My heart was beating so fast as he began to walk toward me. I felt weak in the knees and actually thought I was going to pass out. He came up to me and asked me to dance. While we were dancing, we did the usual introductions of name, rank, and serial number. His name was Michael, and he was a senior – a first-year senior on a five-year plan. Thoughts raced through my head that this guy was at the freshman dance looking for some fresh meat. Nevertheless, he gave me his phone number at his off-campus apartment and told me that he already knew the phone number at Kennedy. Later that night, I saw him dancing with another girl who I later found out was his ex-girlfriend. It was a slow dance, and he looked like he was really into it. I remember feeling jealous but thinking, *how stupid of me.* I barely even knew his name.

Nevertheless, Michael and I soon started dating and became inseparable. I was a freshman and felt as if I had a prized catch, dating a very good-looking senior. It was convenient that he had an apartment and a car. I was able to spend a lot of time off campus and had the use of his car to go wherever I needed to go. His car was a manual shift, and he taught me how to drive it late at night in the parking lot of a mall. Shifting gears was fun to me, and I knew that the first car I bought would be a manual shift. And it was.

Michael was a little shy back in our college days and wasn't as popular as one would have thought based on his looks. On the other hand, I had become fairly well known as a majorette. Even if people didn't know my name, I would be described as the "majorette with the long hair from Florida." Many people got to know Michael through me. Michael was a foreign-language major and would speak French to me sometimes. It would make my heart melt. I've always loved the French language and think it's the most romantic of all languages. He was also in ROTC and was to be a commissioned officer in the army upon graduating from Hampton.

Before I knew it, we were in love, but I was still struggling with my feelings for Herb. He and I were still keeping in touch via letters and phone calls. He wasn't really dating anyone seriously at the time, and I felt guilty that I had fallen for someone else. I felt as if I was outgrowing Herb in some ways, but I was somewhat confused about what I was feeling. He was like an addiction that I didn't want to give up completely. But by the end of my freshman year, I told him that I was in a serious relationship with someone else. I told him that I still cared for him a great deal, and that he would always have a special place in my heart. I never wanted to hurt him, but I think he was a little hurt anyway, even though he said that he understood how I felt. At the time, I think he was wrestling with his own feelings regarding me.

While my personal life was changing, I was being introduced to my first experience as a professional. The president of Hampton, Dr. William Harvey, was visiting our dorm one day. He was a very handsome man. I don't know why he singled me out, but after a brief conversation with him, he asked me if I wanted an on-campus job working in his office. Of course, this was an offer I couldn't refuse, and I took the job and worked in his office as a receptionist throughout my years at Hampton. Working in the president's office was a great experience for me and gave me the opportunity to see all the inner workings of the administration of a college. The seed was planted by that experience that I could get used to and enjoy being in a position of power or around people in power, even if the power wasn't my own. Dr. Harvey became somewhat of a surrogate father for me while I was at Hampton. But the rumors were rampant that he and I had a thing going on. That was very hurtful, as he was never anything but aboveboard with me. While he had a somewhat flirtatious personality, and quite candidly I did too, there was never even a hint of any desire to have an inappropriate relationship. He had a beautiful wife and kids and was just an awesome role model as far as I was concerned. It was an early lesson to me that when people can't rationalize how you got a job, they assume that you must have been sleeping with the boss.

By sophomore year, I felt like attending Hampton was the best decision I could have ever made for myself. I loved being there and had grown to feel quite comfortable. Being a small college, we were like family. If we didn't know everyone's name, we at least knew the face. Our professors got to know us on a personal level. We weren't just a number to them. They took a special interest in each of us and were very aware of each individual's capabilities. They pushed us hard and kept us challenged.

They did a lot more than teach academics to us. In many ways, they gave us lessons on life. They thoroughly prepared us for life outside of the gates of Hampton, our "home by the sea," as we called it. They reminded us that most of us would leave Hampton and enter corporate America, which would look vastly different than Hampton. We would not be in the majority in corporate America; we would be in the minority. They taught us about adapting and knowing when and how to conform without losing our values and our beliefs.

Nerissa and I moved to another girl's dorm, Harkness Hall, during our sophomore year. I really didn't spend very much time there though, because by then Michael and I were quite serious, and I stayed at his apartment frequently. I never agreed to move in and rationalized that as long as I had a room on campus where all my belongings were, I was just spending the night at Michael's – even if it was almost every night. I was doing really well in my classes and had gained a reputation of being pretty smart. I had ended my freshman year making almost all A's, and my sophomore year followed the same trend.

Nerissa and I spent less time together, and she began venturing out making new friends that would eventually become my friends by default. Valerie and Nancy were two such friends. Nerissa and Valerie discovered that they were distant cousins. Val was from Orlando, Florida, and was a very easy-going person who had a very nurturing way about her. As Nerissa and I grew apart, it was Val who picked up the role of looking after Nerissa.

Nancy was from Silver Spring, Maryland, and was always very comical to me, although she probably didn't think of herself in that way. She just had these funny expressions she would use that would make me crack up. She was the only person I ever met that reminded me of the Ivory Snow girl, until later in my IBM career when I met another great friend, Terri, who I placed in this same category. Nancy and I were like night and day but shared many of the same values. She was about as down to earth and natural as you could get. Back then, she wore no makeup and was not really into fashion or appearance. The thought of spending more than five minutes to get dolled up was incomprehensible to Nancy. In some ways, she acted more like one of the guys than one of the girls. I don't mean that in a masculine way – she just could hang with the guys and relate to them without any flirtatious or sexual connotations. And they adored her.

Nancy was probably one of the last people that I thought would have ended up being one of my closest lifetime friends, but that is exactly what happened. She was very easygoing and always appeared comfortable with herself. Perhaps, this had something to do with the fact that she grew up as an only child. Nancy ended up being the one friend I could really pour my heart out to and who was there for me in my time of despair. I think God put her in my life for a reason. She listens and she's nonjudgmental, but she tells it like it is. She doesn't just say what she thinks you want to hear; she says what you need to hear in the pure nakedness of truth.

Throughout college, I had several friends and being part of a sorority was never really that important to me. However, I decided to pledge Alpha Kappa Alpha (AKA), mostly to follow in my sister, Berthina's, footsteps. Pledging was pure hell, and I would often think to myself, *why am I doing this?* The whole thing was somewhat superficial to me, but pledging was an interesting experience in the psychology of human dynamics, if nothing else. I did go on to become dean of pledges my junior year, and I enjoyed that. After all, I was in control, the one calling the shots. I was in my element. That leadership instinct had kicked in.

Michael graduated from Hampton at the end of my sophomore year. He was commissioned in the U. S Army as a second lieutenant in military intelligence and was sent to Tucson, Arizona, for training. He then was to be stationed at Fort Ord, in Monterey, California. We had agreed that we would casually date other people, but we were starting to talk seriously about what the future might hold for the two of us. I think we both knew that our being apart while I finished college would be a big test of our relationship.

Between my junior and senior year at Hampton, I had a summer internship working for IBM in sales and marketing in an Orlando, Florida, branch office. After about a week in the job, I was already hooked on IBM. I loved the people, the technology, and everything that IBM stood for. "IBMers" just seemed to have this unique quality about them. They just seemed to be in a league of their own. Everybody from the branch manager down to the janitor just had this jubilant look – the look of being proud of who they were and where they worked. A look of success no matter what their job was. There were mostly males in the office, and let's just say that I had no problem having any of them wanting to take me under his wing and show me the ropes. I had a great time and was fascinated by the world of sales and marketing of computers. The summer zoomed by, and I knew that IBM was where I wanted to work if I was going to work in corporate America. However, I did have this hidden desire to go to law school and was torn about whether to pursue that desire or not.

Michael and I got engaged the Christmas of my junior year. We had set January 2, 1982, as our wedding date. I had enough credits to graduate from college magna cum laude a semester early, so we decided to get married upon my graduation. Yet, I knew deep in my heart that neither of us was really ready to make that kind of lifetime commitment. We were so young and hadn't even really begun to experience life as young adults. I still had this burning desire to go to law school but kept it hidden from almost everyone. Michael and I were in love. Marriage just seemed like the logical next step for two people in love. We both got caught up in the idea of marriage, and neither of us thought about the reality of what we were doing.

At the completion of my internship with IBM, I received an offer for a permanent job in the Orlando branch to start immediately after graduation. I informed my manager that I was getting married to an army officer and would be living in Monterey, California. The manager agreed to send my file out to the branch office in Monterey and see if they could hire me. The Monterey office was a small satellite office and was a top pick for older sales reps who were almost ready for retirement. The probability of their wanting to take on a young, inexperienced, fresh-out-of-college new hire was remote, but he committed to see what he could do. He told me that San Jose was another option, and while it would be a long commute from Monterey, it was doable.

On the last day of my internship, the branch office had a lunch party for me. I was leaving with a lot of mixed emotions. I had made so many friends, and I liked Orlando a lot. I really did want to go back there to work permanently, but my decision to get married had made that impossible. I hugged everyone and said goodbye. The branch manager informed me that my file was already out on the west coast and that I would hear from someone soon. He told me not to worry about anything – that it would all work out. I pulled out of the IBM parking lot with tears in my eyes and a lot of questions and uncertainty about my future.

I can only imagine that those same sorts of tears and uncertainty about the future were consuming my daughter's mind the day the escort service pulled out of our driveway with her in the car.

CHAPTER FIVE

Smart, But Oh So Naïve

All my life, I've been told that I'm smart, intelligent, and bright – all the nice accolades that would suggest I have the potential and capability to do just about anything that I put my mind to. But nobody ever told me just how naïve I was. In fact, there have been a few incidents in my life that have made me question my own intelligence. I can now rationalize these incidents as a testament to my belief that most people really are good people who mean no harm. Yet, as I mentioned, I was always very trusting and early on developed this warped view that nothing bad would or could ever happen to me. But I was very lucky and blessed because the incidents I will share with you could have turned out very differently, and I may not have lived to share them.

During the summer break between my sophomore and junior year of college, I was back home in Miami and was working for a landscaping company doing some bookkeeping and general office management work. I walked out to my car at the end of a great day and was in a particularly good mood. It was still light outside, but the sun was setting and had cast a beautiful orange glow over the skyline. As I approached my car, I saw a man who looked to be in his late twenties walking toward me. I noticed he had a rather deep voice as he said, "You are so beautiful. Have you ever thought about doing some modeling?"

I smiled and said, "Thank you very much. Actually, I have done a little modeling." He handed me a business card that said "Professional Photographer."

"I would love to take some photos of you and give them to the agency I work for. You have such an exotic look – you can make a fortune," he stated. "Where's your car?"

Without any hesitation at all, I unlocked my car door and got in the driver's seat as he took the front passenger seat. Not once did I even think that this guy was anything other than a photographer. He took a pen from out of his pocket and began scribbling something on the back of his business card.

He said, "The pictures I will take of you will have this kind of effect on men."

He then unzipped his pants and pulled out his erect penis, grabbing my hand to touch it. Without the least bit of fear, I pulled my hand away from his grip and said, "I'm not interested in the kind of pictures you're talking about. Please get out of my car. I have to go."

"Oh, come on, don't you want to have a little fun? I'm going to make you rich," he declared.

Very calmly but firmly I responded, "I've had all the fun I'm going to have. I want you to get out of my car NOW."

He zipped his pants, opened the door, and said, "Call me if you change your mind." He left his business card on the dashboard as he got out of the car. I cranked up my car and almost hit him as I backed out. I drove away and watched him laughing in the reflection of my rearview mirror. It wasn't until I had reached a traffic light that the reality of what had just happened hit me. I broke down crying, ripped up his card, and threw it out the window. It was as if I was telling myself that ripping up the card and throwing it away meant that it had never happened.

I never told anyone about that day. Over the next few weeks following that incident, I was extremely frightened. I had bad dreams about the man, and, in my dreams, he raped me and strangled me to death, leaving my body on the side of the road. It made me feel as if it was a sign of what could have happened to me. Once again, I was lucky and blessed. It's been over 20 years since that little escapade occurred, and every now and then I still have the same dream about "Mr. Photographer."

It was my very first business trip alone with IBM. I was 22 years old, a programmer in San Jose, California, and had been with IBM for about a year-and-a-half. There was a project in Tampa, Florida, that required some extra programming skills, and I was sent to help out. After putting in a long day at the Tampa office, I returned to my hotel. I wasn't hungry because I had eaten a late lunch, but I was a little bored sitting in my hotel room alone. I decided that I would go sit in the bar, have a glass of wine, and perhaps meet some other folks traveling on business that I could talk to.

Upon entering the bar, I felt a little out of place, for this was brand new territory for me. This was my first time ever going to a bar alone. I looked around and there were mostly white males, most of whom looked old enough to be my father. I took a seat at the bar next to a fairly nice looking gentleman who looked to be in his late forties. He was balding and attired in a dark suit with his tie loosened around his neck. I heard him order a glass of Merlot, so I ordered the same. I wasn't very familiar with wines at that point in my life, but I figured he knew what he was doing, so Merlot sounded good to me. He and I exchanged the normal "Hi. How are you?" chitchat. After we both had been served our glasses of wine he asked, "So, are you a working girl?"

I proudly said, "Yes, I'm a working girl". Of course, I was thinking, *I'm a working girl. I work for IBM.*

He then asked, "So what does a girl like you get paid?"

Even though I thought that asking me about my salary was rather personal, I proudly responded, "$26,000 a year."

"You look like a girl who would be worth a lot more than that, but what will a couple of hours cost me?"

It wasn't until *that* statement that the light bulb came on for me and I realized that this guy thought I was a prostitute! I was still in my work attire - a white blouse with a bow tie, a knee length blue skirt, and blue pumps. I looked him right in the eye and very politely said, "I think you misunderstood me. I'm a working girl because I work for IBM."

His face turned as red as a beet. He went on to tell me how sorry he was and how embarrassed he was; he asked me to forgive him for insulting me. While I thought about slapping his face and walking out – and would have felt totally justified in doing so – I instead sat there for the next hour engaged in a very intellectual conversation with him. I never asked him what on earth gave him the impression I was a hooker but came to the conclusion that it was quite stereotypical. I was a young black woman who walked into a bar full of white men alone. Why in the world would I do that unless I was looking to make some money by selling my body? It was shallow, it was hurtful, and it was a rude awakening to the prejudices of the world.

I finished my glass of wine, and he insisted on paying for it. When I got up to leave, he once again told me how sorry he was. He told me how much he enjoyed talking to me, that I was a beautiful person, and that I was going to go far in life. I said good night and walked out. The next evening when I returned to my room after another long day at the office, a dozen roses had been delivered to my room. The card said, "I can never say I'm sorry enough times. You are an amazing young woman. Enjoy the rest of your stay in Tampa." The card wasn't signed. I never saw him at the hotel for the rest of my stay, but I never went back in the bar again either.

My life definitely was impacted by the "working girl" incident. In fact, I still will not go to a bar alone. When I travel on business, I always order room service if I don't have dinner plans with someone. It's funny to me now that I was so naïve and had not a clue what "a working girl" really meant. Even though I had only been with IBM for a very short time, I was already very proud to be an "IBMer." And that night in the bar, I wanted that man to know that I indeed was "a working girl!"

My commute to my first job with IBM was a long one from - Monterey, to San Jose, California, about 60 miles one way. I had an Alpha Romeo convertible and loved to drive with the top down, music blasting with my hair blowing in the wind. I was barely 21 years old and thought I was on top of the world. As I drove home from work one evening, there was a hitchhiker on the side of the road who looked like he could have played the part of Jesus in the Broadway musical *Jesus Christ Superstar*. Without much thought, I pulled over and asked, "Where are you headed?"

"Monterey," he replied.

"Great, that's where I'm going. Get in."

He sat very quietly as I drove, and we didn't say anything to each other. Again, no thoughts entered my mind that he was anything other than a hippie looking for a ride. As I approached my exit, I said, "The next exit is mine, so I'm going to let you off there."

"No you're not," he said.

"But this is my exit, so I need to let you off," I asserted.

"No, I want you to keep driving."

"Ah, okay, if I'm going to keep driving tell me where I'm driving to."

"I don't know. I just want you to keep driving."

I hit my brakes really hard, and the car behind me swerved to keep from rear-ending me. I screamed to the top of my lungs, "Get the hell out of my car, psycho!"

"Okay, okay, I'm getting out. I was just teasing you," he declared. He got out of my car and yelled, "You're a crazy bitch!"

I sped off flipping him the finger. Once again, it was as if a guardian angel was watching over me and allowed me to cheat danger yet again.

I've often wondered if my not being afraid in any of these situations is why I was able to get out of them without getting hurt or even killed. Or perhaps it was because I always had so many people praying for me – namely, my mom. Maybe, it was just luck. Needless to say, I've never picked up another hitchhiker, and I wouldn't dare let a stranger get in my car. I'm much more cautious of people now, maybe even in a paranoid sort of way. But while cautious, I still generally trust people and always want to give them the benefit of the doubt. I still think that most people are good people. I still have a hard time comprehending how or why any person would intentionally harm another person. I'm certainly smart enough to know that it happens and have lived long enough to hear about it happening every day in our society. But in many ways I'm still naïve because I still can't imagine it ever happening to me, even though I've had several brushes with danger.

In many ways, I see a lot of these characteristics in my oldest daughter. She, like me, had a feeling of invincibility, of immortality, and the thought that nothing bad would or could ever happen to her. How wrong we both were.

CHAPTER SIX

Walking Down the Aisle and Making a New Life

My last semester at Hampton was pure craziness. I was taking a full load of classes so I could graduate early, I was planning a wedding, and I was working three jobs. That's right, as if I didn't already have enough on my plate, I took on two additional jobs while keeping my receptionist job in the President's office. I had a job tutoring and a job in a local barbershop as a shampoo girl and cashier. I also did some occasional babysitting for some friends of our family. I was practically a nut case that last semester, but I held it together as I would later learn to do so many more times in my life.

Nerissa and I were still roommates and were living in a coed dorm called The Modulars that resembled a studio apartment. Our friendship was going through a rough period then. I was so consumed in my own little world that I didn't have much time to worry about what was going on with Nerissa. She was having her own personal crises, and I wasn't really there for her. I think it was very bittersweet for her. I was leaving her, graduating early from college with honors and getting married. It appeared like everything in my life was falling in place like a fairy tale. I can imagine that it's hard to live with someone who seems to be floating on clouds all the time while you're feeling like life is full of challenges. But she was a real friend and tried to appear happy for me, even if her true feelings may have been otherwise during that period.

Michael had already moved to Monterey and found a nice condo for us to rent. Most of our conversations revolved around plans for our wedding. What he wanted and what my parents wanted weren't exactly in sync. I often felt caught between my husband-to-be and my parents, which is not a good position to be in. But they were footing the bill, so in the end they got their way. We were planning a rather large wedding with 32 people in our wedding party. Secretly, I thought about just nixing the wedding and eloping. But how could I deny my father the opportunity to walk his baby girl down the aisle and hand her off to the man who she was supposed to spend the rest of her life with? There was not a chance that I could do that to him and live with myself. It seemed like Michael and I spent more time arguing about than planning our future. I was really having second thoughts about marriage, and I think he was too. But we were so caught up in the planning of the wedding that we were too blind to see that neither of us was prepared for marriage.

I was also a little stressed out because, while I had heard from IBM on the west coast, I still didn't have a firm job offer in hand. What I had was an invitation to come in for an interview once I moved to Monterey. I felt confident that I would get a job with them, but it was still uncomfortable to not know for certain. Fortunately, I had interviewed with some other major corporations and did have two other job offers. However, I wasn't that interested in either of the other offers, but at least I had a contingency plan just in case IBM didn't come through.

I also was still struggling with whether or not I was really over Herb. I thought I was, but I knew I still had some feelings for him. Rationalizing what those feeling were was a struggle for me. We had maintained contact and were very good friends. I wasn't sure if I loved him like a brother or as a lover. After all, we had grown up practically like brother and sister, and our love evolved over time as we grew up. In many ways, it was like a blossoming flower bud. It was so innocent, so beautiful, and so pure. He had another girlfriend by then and was going to be a pilot and commissioned officer in the U. S Air Force upon graduating from Florida State University.

I kept all of my unresolved feelings and my uncertainty about marrying Michael tucked deep inside. Come hell or high water, we were getting married. All the wedding plans had been completed, and the big day was just around the corner. I'll never forget the day before the wedding. Michael and I were fighting like cats and dogs. My mom told me we could call it off, that it wasn't too late. While my family adored Michael, they did not think that we were ready for marriage. But I said, "There's no way I'm calling it off. I'm getting married tomorrow. We'll be fine. It's just premarital jitters."

Since I was very close to Herb's family, I had asked his brothers to be in the wedding, and they agreed. I had more girls in the wedding than Michael had guys, so we needed two more escorts. Michael actually had gotten to know Herb's family over the years and was very fond of them. He even liked Herb and always described him as a very nice, all American guy. In fact, Herb's parents had a pool party and cookout at their home for Michael and me and our wedding party the day before the wedding. Michael's best man was supposed to be his cousin, Whit, who was a doctor in the air force.

At the very last minute, Whit had to work and was not able to get a flight out in time to make it to the wedding. Ironically, Whit and Herb were almost the same size, so Whit's rented tux fit Herb. While there was no way Michael was going to ask Herb to be his best man, he asked him if he would be in the wedding. Being the very nice guy that Herb was and always had been, he accepted the offer.

Walking down the aisle on my father's arm, I felt as if I was in another world. Tears were streaming down my face, and everyone thought I was crying because I was so happy. But I was crying because I knew I was making the biggest mistake of my life. I knew I wasn't ready for marriage, and I knew Michael wasn't ready either. I looked at the wedding party, and my eyes met Herb's. He had a very blank look on his face. While I had no idea what was going through his mind, I knew what was going through mine – utter emotional conflict. Nevertheless, once we reached the altar and I looked into Michael's eyes, there was a look of love and admiration that melted my heart. I snapped back into reality and accepted the fact that I was going to be his wife. I convinced myself that it was all going to be okay, that we would have an "Endless Love," which was the theme of our wedding, and that we would live happily ever after.

Michael and I did not have a formal honeymoon. We decided that we would drive my car across the country to California, stopping many places on the way. We did have a lot of fun on the trip, and we were very much in love. It was much more romantic than I had envisioned a driving honeymoon could be. By the time we reached our various destinations, we were so tired that we just wanted to get into bed and do what honeymooners do, versus taking in any sights. We talked a lot, laughed a lot, and sang, and he told me how much he loved me in all the various languages he could speak. We were very comfortable with each other and, despite all the uncertainty I felt previously, I now thought that we were going to be just fine.

Finally, we reached Monterey, which was so beautiful that I knew I was going to love living there. I had to learn the role of an officer's wife and get indoctrinated into military life. While we lived in a condo off base, we spent a lot of time on the base at military functions. Everyone quickly welcomed me with open arms and thought that Michael and I were about as close to Ken and Barbie as you could get. The other officers' wives from his unit took me under their wings, as I was the youngest wife and definitely the most naïve.

I went for my interview at IBM in San Jose about a week after arriving in Monterey. Right away, I was confused as to why I was interviewing with the Field Engineering Division, as my interest was sales and marketing. Somehow, the Field Engineering office had received my file instead of the sales and marketing branch office. Despite the fact that I had no programming background, they thought I had the aptitude and capability to be a great programmer. As it turned out, the job they were considering me for was a Level 2 JES 3 programmer. This was a job that they had never hired kids right out of college for. Typically, you would be a program support rep (PSR) and then get promoted into this job. But they were running a pilot program and wanted to hire a few "smart kids" straight out of college to see if they could train them to do this job successfully. I really had no interest in being a programmer, but they made me a great job offer and I accepted.

That first year of marriage was blissful. In fact, it was almost storybook like. After renting a condo for a short period of time, Michael and I bought our own brand new condo. We bought a new Alpha Romeo sports convertible, and we were very happy building a home together. We were young, in love, and becoming successful. He was doing well as an officer, and I was enjoying my programming job. We were making really good money, and it appeared that life couldn't get much better than this. We had many friends inside and outside of the military and always had some social function to go to. Sometimes I felt like my life was a dream come true. Little did I know that it was all about to change.

A few months after our first anniversary, Michael started hanging out with the guys more and more. We were starting to do more things apart than together. We began arguing about everything, and it was apparent that we were growing apart. Michael was staying out later and later at night with inconsistent stories of his whereabouts. I began suspecting that he was having an affair. After finding an earring in our bed that did not belong to me, I confronted him and he came clean. My worst nightmare was confirmed and I was crushed, angry, and felt betrayed. He told me, "I love you very much. But we're so young. Maybe we shouldn't have gotten married so soon." I responded sarcastically, "Oh – thanks for telling me this now." All those feelings of uncertainty I had prior to our wedding were coming back to haunt me. He agreed to go to marriage counseling, and I agreed to try to forgive him for his indiscretion.

We had a great marriage counselor, and some of our sessions were actually a little comical. Michael would talk about how much he loved me and how I had everything that any man would want in a wife. He would say, "Lisa's not the problem. There's absolutely nothing wrong with her. It's just that I don't want to be married anymore." After multiple sessions with this same dialogue, the marriage counselor asked to speak to me alone. I'll never forget what he told me. He said that he could keep taking our money and have us to continue coming back week after week, but that marriage counseling was only effective when two people realize there's a problem that they both want to work on. He said that since Michael consistently claimed that there was no problem other than the realization that he did not want to be married, there was nothing to work with. He put his hand on my shoulder and looked me right in the eyes. He said, "Lisa, you're young, intelligent, and beautiful. There are no kids from this marriage, and you can walk away with very little difficulty. Move on with your life and don't ever look back."

It was extremely difficult to accept the reality of the marriage counselor's statement. I tried to hang in there for a few more months with Michael, and things were getting a little better. However, I became extremely ill one night and was rushed to the hospital by ambulance and hospitalized in intensive care. They weren't sure what was wrong with me, but I had an irregular heartbeat, tightness in the chest, and difficulty breathing. Based on my symptoms, the doctors thought that I had suffered a mild heart attack but didn't want to conclude that as a diagnosis because I was only 23 and in very good physical shape. After a week in the hospital, I came home. Michael stayed home from work that first day and took care of me. My second day home, he told me he was going to work and would come home during lunch to check on me. He didn't come back until late that night. To this day, I have no idea where he was or what had happened, but when he came home and walked in the door, he simply said, "Lisa, I really love you, but I can't do this anymore. I don't want to be married."

As physically weak as I was, I think I actually went a little insane and just lost it. I was totally out of control with rage, and I think Michael thought I was going to kill him and then kill myself. I'm sure I scared the hell out of him. I was so out of control that I scared myself too. Michael called our neighbor Delois, who was a friend of ours and also a nurse. She came over, gave me a Valium, and took me back to her place. I called my mom sobbing and told her that I needed to come home for a while to get myself together. My mother talked to me for a long time on the phone telling me how much she loved me and that no man was worth destroying myself over. She prayed with me and told me I was going to be fine, to pull myself together. She talked to Delois and asked her to please get me on the next plane leaving for Miami.

When I arrived in Miami, my family was devastated by what they saw. I had lost so much weight that I looked anorexic. I had not brushed my hair in days and was wearing no makeup. I looked like walking death. My entire family was there for me with all the love and support I needed. It validated to me that my family would always be there for me no matter what. That solid foundation of unconditional love and prayer that I had grown up with was surrounding me. My family was nursing me back to health physically, emotionally, and spiritually. I never once heard, "We told you not to get married."

One day Berthina took me in the bathroom and told me to look at myself in the mirror. She said the girl in the mirror was not who I was. She told me to reach deep within my soul and pull out that fighting spirit and get myself together. She told me I had too much going for me to let this destroy me and no matter how hopeless things seemed at the moment, brighter days were just around the corner. I didn't know then that many years later we would have a similar conversation under different circumstances. I made up my mind at that moment to accept what the marriage counselor had told me months earlier. I decided I was going to go back to California, file for divorce from Michael, move on with my life, and never look back. And that's exactly what I did.

Moving on and never looking back is a hard lesson that I pray my daughter has learned. We all have choices in life. We can choose to stay stuck and be miserable, or we can choose to make significant changes in our lives, moving on without ever looking back.

CHAPTER SEVEN

A Free but Wild Butterfly

I always felt that IBM was a great company and had a great deal of concern and respect for its employees. These feelings were validated during this first major crisis in my life. I was blessed to have a female manager, even though my department was almost all men. When I returned to California, I told my manager I was getting divorced and that there was no reason for me to stay on the West Coast. I asked if it would be possible for me to transfer as quickly as possible somewhere on the East Coast so that I could be closer to my family. She asked me where I wanted to go. I hadn't really given much thought to this, but out of the blue I said, "Atlanta." I had only been to Atlanta a few times in my life, but I had heard great things about the city. It had a reputation of being a Mecca for young black professionals. I had maintained sporadic contact with a manager I had met while interning with IBM in Orlando and who was now in Atlanta. I gave my manager his name, and she said that she would get in touch with him to see if there were any opportunities in Atlanta. I told her that while I liked being a programmer, I wasn't passionate about it and would prefer to get into sales and marketing.

They say that timing is everything, and timing definitely was on my side. As it turned out, the Atlanta branch office was looking for people who knew MVS, an operating system that I was very familiar with. They were looking for System Engineers (SEs), which are sort of like technical sales reps. My programming background was a great foundation for me to transition easily into the SE role. I flew to Atlanta to interview with the branch manager, Mike McCarthy, and we hit it off great. He told me that I would be great as a sales rep (they were called marketing reps back then) or an SE. But he really needed SEs, so he asked me if I would take the job. I told him I would be thrilled. He said he needed a few weeks to work out the logistics of getting me transferred, but he would get me there as soon as possible.

I went back to California and was excited about the opportunity for a new start. I wanted to move out of the condo I shared with Michael while I waited for my transfer to get worked out. While we were very cordial to each other under the circumstances, it was too painful to stay in the same house with him. Several of my female colleagues who had become my good friends were literally fighting over which one of them I would stay with. I ended up splitting my time between staying with a single colleague who also was named Lisa and a married friend named Nancy. They were wonderful to me and literally took care of me. I'll never forget them and what they did for me.

I flew back to Atlanta over a weekend to find a place to stay. The cost of living in Atlanta was very inexpensive compared to California. I found an attractive large three-bedroom apartment to rent in a nice complex in an area of Atlanta called Sandy Springs. I didn't need a place that large, but it was very affordable for me and I decided to take it. I was glowing with excitement because this was going to be my first time really living on my own. After all, I had gone from my parents' house to college and then right into marriage. I was so busy making plans to move that I don't think the reality of what was really happening had actually hit me. It wasn't until the day that the movers came to pack my things that it hit me – and Michael too – that I was really leaving. That it was the end of our marriage. That the "endless love" had ended. I vividly remember standing outside in the driveway of our condo with Michael as the movers drove my car onto the moving van. Michael had tears streaming down his face and said, "You're really leaving aren't you? I love you so much, Lisa, and I'm so sorry it all turned out this way. You were the last person I ever wanted to hurt. I will always love you." I was crying too, and we embraced each other so tightly that we could both barely breathe. I whispered in his ear, "It's okay. I will always love you too, but we're both going to be okay."

I left for Atlanta for good a few days later. I felt like a butterfly that was set free to explore life from a different vantage point. I was scared but excited. This was a new chapter in my life, and I was determined that it would be a great one. I knew it would take me a long time to get over Michael or to ever trust another man again. But I also knew that I loved being in love and that I would eventually love again. I had a feeling that somewhere in Atlanta my black knight in shining armor was waiting to find me, and when he did, we would both know. But another relationship was the last thing I needed at the moment. This was my time to focus on me.

Before I left for Atlanta, my mom gave me the phone number of Greg, the son of an old family friend who lived in the city. Greg and I had not seen each other since we were about 12 years old, when my family visited his in New York. We considered ourselves cousins when we were young even though we were not really related. My mom told me that Greg's father had informed him that I was moving to Atlanta and that Greg would help me get settled and show me around. The last time Greg had seen me, I was still wearing pigtails and had braces, and he had a big Afro. It was comforting to know that right away I would have at least one person in Atlanta whom I knew and could trust.

Being the anal and almost obsessively organized person that I am, I had already arranged for all of my utilities and phone to be turned on prior to my arrival. My furniture and car were scheduled to be delivered the day after my arrival. When I got to my new apartment, I had a very strange and empty feeling. There's nothing like being in a large apartment alone with no furniture. In retrospect, a hotel room for the night might have been a wiser choice, but I was determined to spend my first night in Atlanta in my very own place – as empty as it was. I walked into each room and mentally decided where and how all my furniture would be placed. I drove to a nearby Kmart and bought a cordless phone, a pillow, and a blanket. I went back to my apartment, sat in the middle of the living room floor, and began sobbing uncontrollably. Reality had set in that I was on my own and that I was responsible for my own happiness. It was an extremely lonely feeling. I called my mom to let her know that I was as settled as I could be for the night. I told her that I was fine, but I knew she knew differently and that she was extremely worried about me. After I hung up the phone, I placed my pillow and blanket in the middle of my bedroom floor and cried myself to sleep.

The next morning, the movers knocking on my door awakened me. They arrived a little earlier than I expected, and it didn't take them very long to get the truck unloaded. I spent the rest of the morning and afternoon unpacking boxes and getting myself organized. By that evening, I was exhausted and realized that I hadn't eaten all day or didn't have any food in the house. I decided to take a shower and go grocery shopping and thought I'd call Greg when I returned. I remember walking around my apartment after I was cleaned up, talking out loud to myself and saying, "This is home now."

I called Greg after I returned from my shopping excursion, and he was excited to hear from me. He had been expecting my call. He was working as a mortician at a funeral home and was on call that evening, meaning that he could come see me but would have to leave if he got a call to pick up a dead body. I told him we could wait until the next day, but he said he couldn't wait to see me. He asked me jokingly if I still was wearing pigtails and braces. I laughed and assured him that the pigtails and braces were gone. He assured me that his Afro was gone as well. I knew by the excitement in both of our voices that we each were curious to see how the other one had turned out.

Waiting for Greg to arrive was like waiting for water to boil. I paced around my apartment like a teenager anxiously anticipating the arrival of a first date. I mentally pictured what Greg would look like now. The sudden knock at the door startled me, and my heart felt as if it skipped a beat. I opened the door, and Greg and I looked at each other and broke out into huge smiles. We hugged each other, and he said, "Wow! You're more beautiful than I imagined!" He came into my apartment, and we immediately started to catch up. He had grown up to be quite handsome and was doing well for himself. I was impressed that he had followed his childhood dream of becoming a mortician. When we were kids, he would talk about wanting to be a mortician. I couldn't imagine why anyone would want to work with dead people, but I supposed someone had to do it. I was intrigued with his line of work and asked a million questions. He told me that he would take me to the funeral home and show me around. Honestly, I wasn't really excited about that offer, but my curiosity got the best of me and I said, "That would be awesome."

After catching up on family and each other's careers, our conversation moved into our love lives. Greg recently had broken up with a girlfriend and wasn't really dating anyone seriously. He was very interested in what happened with my marriage. It was apparent that we had an instant attraction to each other and that we felt very comfortable together. He offered to show me around Atlanta and was already making plans for some things we could do together. After visiting with me for a few hours, he got paged to go to the morgue to pick up a body. He told me he would call me later that night. He kissed me on the cheek, told me how great it was to see me, and said that he was looking forward to us spending time together. He left, and I thought, *life in Atlanta is going to be okay.*

The morning of my first day in the Atlanta office was filled with much excitement and anticipation. I hadn't slept very well the night before because my adrenaline was running fast and furiously. I think I actually looked at my alarm clock every hour as if trying to force it to go off. I finally just got out of the bed at 5:00 AM, well before I needed to. I made some coffee and went over my driving directions to the office for the hundredth time. Even though I had set my clothes out the night before, I decided that morning that I didn't like what I had selected, so I went into a frenzy of trying on several different suits before I settled on one – a very basic navy blue suit. After I showered and dressed, I went into a cleaning tirade, ensuring all of the clothes I had strewn all over the bed were carefully hung back up in the closet. I'd always had a pet peeve about leaving my home tidy so everything would be in its place when I returned.

Once I was en-route to the office, I quickly realized that I had misjudged the amount of traffic in Atlanta. Fortunately, I had given myself plenty of time, but the traffic made me anxious. I arrived at the office, and, once I walked inside, I felt as if I had died and gone to heaven. I had come from a work environment of predominantly older white males. The Atlanta office was quite diverse from a gender, age, and racial perspective. I knew right away that I was going to really enjoy this new atmosphere.

I met with my new manager and took care of some administrative procedures. He introduced me to many of my co-workers and showed me which desk in the "bull pen" was mine. One of the first people I got to know well was Pam. She too was black and single, and although she was a few years older than me, we had this instant connection. She invited me to join her for lunch. As it turned out, Pam had graduated from Hampton a few years ahead of me. We both realized what a small world it was when we discovered that Tommy, one of the two guys at Hampton that my mom had asked to look out for me, was Pam's brother. I knew that Pam and I would become very good friends, and we did. She remains one of my closest friends even to this day.

I was assigned to work with a senior SE named Gordon. We were to be a team, and I was to work on several of his accounts with him. He and I got along very well, and I knew that I would learn a lot from him. One of our larger customers was Emory University, and Gordon took me to the campus to introduce me to the client. The Emory data processing crew was kind of a young, hip crowd. After meeting several of the folks, I was introduced to

Jim. He was a handsome white male who was my age and had long curly hair. He reminded me of a guy named Calvin I had dated briefly in high school during one of my short breakups with Herb. Actually, I've always had a physical attraction to white guys with curly hair. On the drive back to the branch office, Gordon told me about all of the different personalities of the people I had just met. I casually mentioned to him that I thought Jim was cute. Gordon informed me that Jim had recently gotten married. I remember thinking to myself, *I'm not looking to marry the guy. I just think he's cute.* I certainly didn't imagine in a million years what would happen later.

Over the next several months in Atlanta, I settled very easily into my new life. I loved my job and made many friends inside and outside of IBM. Greg and I hung out frequently together, and our relationship evolved into serious dating. If I wasn't with Greg, I was with Pam. She and I did many things outside of work together and had a blast with each other. It was as if I had known her all my life.

By this time, I had become more familiar with the funeral business than I really cared to. On the nights Greg worked, I would go to the funeral home to keep him company. I watched him embalm a few bodies and found the whole process fascinating. I was amazed that it didn't really bother me to be around dead people. It was very clinical to me. I once asked Greg if it was depressing working with sad families on funeral arrangements all the time. He told me that he had learned how to emotionally detach himself – sort of the same way doctors emotionally detach themselves from terminally ill patients. He said the only time it really bothered him was when it was a child's funeral.

Although there were several accounts that Gordon and I worked on together, Emory had become my favorite. I really liked the people there, and Gordon and I would often go for pizza and beer with them after work. Every Friday, we had status meetings with the data processing team at Emory. We sat at a large table in the conference room to review the status of the various projects we were involved with. Jim and I always sat across the table from each other. Our eyes would meet frequently, and I would smile and look away. It was quite obvious that he and I were attracted to each other, but I dismissed it as a physical attraction and nothing more.

After being in Atlanta for about six months, I became very ill with a severe kidney infection and was hospitalized. Much to my surprise and embarrassment, the folks from Emory came to visit me at the hospital one evening. Greg was also there. I'll never forget what he said when the Emory crew left. "That Jim guy has a thing for you," he asserted.

I said, "No he doesn't. Besides, he's married."

Greg responded, "I don't care if he's married or not – he likes you. I watched him watch you, and, the way he was looking at you, it's pretty obvious he has a thing for you."

After spending four days in the hospital, I was released but was told to have complete bed rest for a week. Greg suggested that he come stay with me at my apartment so he could take care of me while I recuperated. My mom actually thought that this was a good idea. Well, Greg did stay with me, and he did take great care of me. But before I knew it, he had gradually moved in and we were living together – something I was not entirely comfortable with. Our relationship had become serious, but I wasn't sure it had become serious for the right reasons. I was clearly on the rebound from my divorce. I adored Greg, but I knew that he was much more serious than I was. There were many things about him that bothered me, namely that he was extremely jealous and possessive. I knew that he dreamed of owning his own funeral home someday and having his wife work with him in the business. I honestly couldn't picture myself being "the funeral lady."

Over the next few months, all sorts of strange and twisted things happened. Greg and I moved into a townhouse, and he bought me a beautiful engagement ring, which I accepted, even though I knew in my heart I was not going to marry him. Jim's marriage didn't work out, and he was getting divorced. He had gotten a job with IBM and was leaving Emory to move to Albany, Georgia. I met a guy named Mack, the brother of an IBM friend who was ten years older than me and was an attorney. I was totally infatuated with him. Michael and I had started communicating again, as did Herb and I. I clearly felt like a butterfly that was flying aimlessly all over the place.

During this period, I met a woman from a local modeling agency who encouraged me to get my portfolio updated and to start doing some modeling again. I signed on with a modeling agency and was moonlighting as a model. It was a rather interesting contrast – by day a conservative IBMer and in the evenings and on weekends a swimwear and lingerie model. My IBM colleagues quickly discovered my modeling secret when I appeared in a local TV commercial for a department store. The commercial played constantly, so there was no hiding or denying that it was me. I wore jeans and a tee shirt in the commercial, so at least I wasn't appearing all over TV in my underwear! The extra income from modeling was pretty good, but I ended my modeling moonlighting after doing a Valentine's Day lingerie fashion show at the mall. I looked out into the audience and was horrified to see not only one of my IBM customers, but also several of my male colleagues. Even though the lingerie I was modeling was very tasteful and actually covered more of my body than a bikini would, I knew that if I wanted to be taken seriously as an IBM professional, the modeling had to end. And so it did.

Then I had to go to an IBM class for a few weeks in Dallas. It was during this Dallas trip that I think I came to my senses. I didn't want to hurt Greg, but there was no way I was going to make another marriage mistake. I decided that, as soon as I returned to Atlanta, I would break up with Greg and ask him to move out. I could not continue to pretend that I was going to marry him. It wasn't fair to him, and it wasn't fair to me. Every time Greg and I spoke on the phone while I was in Dallas, I think he sensed that something was wrong. But I wasn't going to deliver breakup news over the phone, so I just told him that we had some serious things to talk about when I returned. I think he knew what was coming.

Upon returning to Atlanta from Dallas, I gave Greg the ring back. I broke his heart. He was hurt, and he was angry. He said he felt as if I used him to get over Michael. I tried to explain to him that I did care for him a great deal but that he and I just weren't right for each other. I told him that I was sorry that I hurt him. I could totally understand his feelings because I knew what it felt like to be hurt. I knew that crushing feeling of having the person you love tell you that he doesn't want to be with you anymore. I hoped then that I would never have to be on the giving or receiving end of that kind of conversation again. It wasn't easy and it wasn't pretty, but it had to be done. Greg moved out the next day. He and I didn't speak for a long time afterward, but, like all of my previous relationships, we eventually started communicating again and became friends.

After Greg and I broke up, I'd have to say that I went through my wild period. For the next six months, I was a little out there. During this period, I even went out with a motorcycle cop who had given both Pam and me speeding tickets when I was following her in my car. We went to court, and

I got out of the ticket, but Pam didn't. The officer in turn asked me out to dinner. I went out with him and was totally bored. I called Pam after my date and told her, "The guy was a complete zero!"

Pam said, "That's what you get for being a hussy!"

Mr. Motorcycle cop called me several times after our date, but I never returned his calls. He eventually stopped calling. Mack and I started going out casually. He was tall and handsome, but I was very attracted to his intellect. I liked him very much, but he treated me more like a kid sister than a love interest.

Even though Jim had moved to Albany, Georgia, which is three hours south of Atlanta, he was in Atlanta frequently for IBM training classes. He called me a lot under the auspices of getting information about the training classes, which I had already completed. During one of his Atlanta visits, I agreed to meet him for dinner. Now that he was no longer my customer or married, I figured he might be interesting to hang out with.

I discovered that Jim was not only interesting, but also a lot of fun. We had many things in common. I discovered that we both enjoyed the arts and that he too played the piano. The first time I heard him play, I was totally blown away. He was awesome. After hanging out with him several times, I knew that he and I definitely had a special connection, this chemistry that I had never really felt with anyone else. It was a little scary to me because there was something kind of mysterious about him. It was apparent that we were attracted to each other physically, but the attraction was much deeper than that. It was as if we were attracted to each other's souls. We became very good platonic friends who, at this point, had some deep feelings for each other that neither of us quite knew what to do with.

Jim and I saw each other frequently on his many visits to Atlanta but were still just pals. He and I had never even kissed at this point, even though we had spent a lot of time together. But that soon changed. I remember that first kiss as if it was yesterday. We had gone to visit some friends of his who had worked with him when he was at Emory. I had driven my own car, meeting him at his friend's condo. After spending several hours with his friends, it was getting late and I needed to leave. Jim walked me out to my car. I leaned against the passenger door, as we were consumed in conversation. Then he pulled me to him, and we engaged in the most passionate kiss I had ever experienced. It was as if firecrackers were going off. My body was weak with desire. The naked truth is that I was hoping he would throw me to the ground and make love to me right there by my car! But he was the ultimate gentleman and instead walked me to the driver's side, opened the door, and said good night.

As I drove home, my mind raced with thoughts. Could I actually be falling for Jim? This white guy who I found mysterious and still couldn't quite figure out. After all, I had come to Atlanta to find my black knight in shining armor. Could Jim be my knight in shining armor even though he was the wrong color? Would I let race stop me from perhaps being with the one guy who might actually be my soul mate? Did race matter? Martin Luther King, Jr.'s mantra that my parents constantly reinforced played in my head – "One shouldn't be judged by the color of their skin, but by the content of their character."

I felt like my love life was a tangled web of confusion. I was dating Mack and Jim simultaneously. I really liked Mack but decided we would never be anything more than just good friends. I really liked Jim, but the race factor was always in the back of my mind. Herb and I had actually gotten together once when he visited Atlanta, and we had a great time, but I knew our relationship was past history and that we should leave it at that. I still loved him in a special way but knew I wasn't the right girl for him.

Michael and I were talking frequently and were going to see each other at the wedding of his relative, whom I was quite fond of. It had been almost two years since we had seen each other. He was stationed in Germany and was now a father. He had a son from one of his flings. He had no interest in marrying the mother of his son but did the responsible thing and was very much a part of his child's life. While my love life was a tangled web of confusion, my thoughts would always return to Jim as I would lie in bed at night – alone.

One day, Jim and I went to the annual Atlanta Piedmont Park Arts Festival and had a great time. He casually mentioned that he wanted to go to St. Thomas for the Fourth of July, but a buddy of his had backed out of the trip. He said, "Why don't you go with me?"

I wasn't really sure if he was serious or not, but I said, "If you get a two-bedroom condo and take care of the airfare, I'll take care of the entertainment expenses."

"That's a deal," he responded.

I honestly didn't give it much more thought until he called me several days later and informed me that all the arrangements had been made. My anxiety level skyrocketed. I was about to leave for New Jersey to attend Michael's cousin's wedding and was going to see Michael there. If things went well with Michael, I was planning to extend my trip over the Fourth of July weekend. This was a going to be a major conflict. I called Pam and told her that I didn't know what to do. At this point, other than kissing, there had been no physical contact with Jim. I didn't know if a weekend trip with him would be uncomfortable or not. Pam told me, "Girl, go to St Thomas with Jim and have a great time. If you decide you don't like him, come back and dump him." I told her she was crazy but what the heck – I'd go.

I went to New Jersey, and as soon as I saw Michael, I had those same feelings I had the first time I saw him. You would have never known that we were divorced. It was as if we hadn't missed a beat. All of his relatives were egging us on for a reconciliation. We had a wonderful time together. He told me how much he still loved me and that he was so sorry for everything that happened, and he knew he had made a big mistake. He tried to convince me to come back to Germany with him and give things another try. I was falling fast and hard but was skeptical about dropping everything in my life for Michael after all he had put me through. He asked me to stay in New Jersey over the Fourth of July weekend. I told him I had plans. I came very close to calling Jim and backing out of our St. Thomas trip. But Jim had been too nice to me, and I really cared about him. I knew that if I backed out of the trip, I would always wonder, *what if.* I finally told Michael that I couldn't change my plans. It was great to see him, but I needed time to sort through my feelings. I went back to Atlanta, unpacked, and repacked for St. Thomas.

Jim and I left on an early flight out of Atlanta for St. Thomas. I invited him to stay at my place the night before so we could go to the airport together. He had never stayed at my place during his Atlanta visits, and we had never slept together. When it was time to go to bed, I must admit that it was a little awkward – and I'll just leave it at that!

I was awestruck by the beauty of St. Thomas. We stayed at a condo resort called Mahogany Run. Jim made good on his promise and had gotten a two-bedroom condo. He told me I could have the master bedroom and that he would take the smaller bedroom. After I unpacked, I went into his room and noticed that he had brand new Calvin Kline underwear still in their packaging. I don't know why, but I found this rather cute. Had he actually bought brand new underwear for the occasion? I still tease him about that to this day.

Our St. Thomas trip was about as close to *Fantasy Island* as one could get. It was so romantic. We had an absolutely spectacular time. Jim discovered that I was a great lover of the water and enjoyed swimming and snorkeling. It was another one of the many things that we had in common. I fell in love with Jim on that trip and thought he fell in love with me too. But he tells me that he fell in love with me the moment he first laid eyes on me at Emory. That second bedroom never got used!

Jim and I were married a year later. We knew we were soul mates, and neither of us was going to let race get in the way. If people had a problem with it, we decided that it was their problem, not ours. We were in love, we were happy, and we wanted to spend the rest of our lives together. I went to Atlanta as a free but wild butterfly. I knew that my knight in shining armor would find me. I just never imagined that it would happen the way it did or that he would come in different packaging.

After reflecting back on my relationships with males and even my friendships with females, it's interesting to me that when I meet people, I know right away if there is a special connection or not. Those who I have that instant connection with become long-term relationships. When I met Jim, even though he was my customer and he was married, I used to fantasize about our being together – I just never imagined in my wildest dreams that it would become reality.

Now, as I think about my wild period, I laugh at some of the things I did. I also reflect back and realize how some decisions ultimately changed my life, for better or for worse. Hopefully, years from now, my daughter will look back over her own wild period and be able to laugh – and learn – too.

CHAPTER EIGHT

Blending Races in a Marriage

When Jim and I made the decision to get married, we never really discussed the challenges that an interracial marriage could bring. We were in love and both believed that race didn't matter. Our only discussion relative to kids was that we both wanted at least one. Again, we didn't talk about the challenges that a biracial child might face. We never really thought of it as an issue. After all, this was the late '80s and times had changed...or had they?

Oftentimes, when people from different backgrounds engage in marriage, whether those differences are racial, religious, or socioeconomic - there can be family conflicts, disapproval, or downright disownment. Fortunately, we did not have to deal with that. My family accepted Jim from the start, and while they may have had a few concerns about the social pressures we might face, they were supportive of our decision to marry. Jim's mother and sister had the same attitude. Yet, while his father and brother didn't disapprove, they were less than thrilled when there appeared to be a recast of out *Guess Who's Coming To Dinner*. But once Jim's father met me and got to know me, he liked and accepted me. It took a while for me to grow on his brother, but we eventually became close.

Since we both had big weddings the first time around, we decided not to go down that path again, that we would get married in the chapel on the Emory University campus and would have just the two of us and the minister. We were required by the minister to attend a few premarital counseling sessions, and when we informed him that we would have no guests at our wedding, including our parents, he seemed concerned. I think he initially thought that we were getting married without our parents' blessings. We explained to him that our families were supportive of our decision to get married, but since we both had been married before, this was how we wanted to do it. While Jim's family lived in Atlanta, mine lived in Miami. I didn't want my parents to fly in for a ten-minute ceremony, and there was no way I could have his parents attend if my parents didn't. Every time we thought about inviting a few friends, we ran into the dilemma that if you invite this one person, then you have to invite this other person. It got too complicated, so we stuck with our plan of inviting no one. That is, until we realized that we needed a witness. So in the end, our friend Kin and his wife came to be the witnesses, as well as the photographers. Our wedding was very intimate and very special. This time we did it our way. There were no distractions of pomp and circumstance, and we both said our vows with meaning and conviction.

Jim's parents insisted on having a party for us at their home following our little ceremony. I had already come to know most of Jim's relatives and his parents' close friends, so it was actually a nice little celebration. We left for our honeymoon in Jamaica the next morning and spent our first night as a married couple at the Waverly Hotel. The Waverly is still very special to us, and we stay there occasionally when we go back to Atlanta to visit.

Our trip to Jamaica was a blast, even though neither of us liked it too much when we first arrived. We stayed at a resort in Ochos Rios, and even though we were warned by the hotel staff not to venture away from the resort on our own, that's exactly what we did! We wanted to see Jamaica like natives, not like tourists. We hired a local named Tony to show us around, and he was an awesome tour guide. Some days, we would lie out on the beach, each floating on a raft and getting lost in the sounds of reggae music. Tony suggested that I get my hair braided, something most female tourists do when they go to Jamaica. He took Jim and me to a little village by the beach. He told the girl to braid my hair, and he told me that he and Jim would return for me in a little while. The girl braided my hair so tight that I felt like my eyes were slanting.

When Jim and Tony came back for me, four Jamaican guys showed up, too. One of them asked Jim, "Is that your woman?"

"It sure is," Jim replied.

"You fight for your woman?" Before Jim answered, I broke out in a cold sweat, thinking that these guys were going to try to gang rape me.

My thoughts were interrupted by Jim's response, "You damn right I'll fight for my woman!"

While I was relieved by his response, I was scared to death. But the guy said with typical Jamaican flair, "No problem, man. No problem."

The four guys left, and Jim and I looked at each other. I knew we were both thinking the same thing – *Let's get the hell out of here!* Jim paid the girl who braided my hair, and Tony took us back to our resort. We laughed about that incident for the rest of the trip. Even now, every once in a while, I jokingly ask Jim, "You fight for your woman?"

We made the decision right after we were married that we would just let nature take its course and not use any birth-control methods. While we weren't trying to get pregnant, we weren't trying to prevent it either. But I must admit, every month that went by with my not getting pregnant led to a little disappointment and some concern. Although we never talked about it, I knew that each of us wondered if there was a fertility problem with one of us. We were quite busy with our jobs however, buying our first home together, and building our life with each other.

One thing that sticks out in my memory about our first year of marriage is that I took a lot of heat from my black male friends. While they all liked Jim and accepted him, they would often ask me in private, "Why would a fine sister like you marry a white dude?" My response was always the same. I would say, "I didn't go out looking to marry a white dude. I met and fell in love with a wonderful person who just happened to be white. Why should I let race get in the way of my happiness?" They could never answer that question and would just shake their heads and say, "You're one of a kind, girl."

Over the years we have had some awkward moments in situations where people didn't realize that I was black and would tell racist jokes or make derogatory comments about blacks. Depending on the particular circumstances, we would handle each situation differently. Sometimes I would comment, "I happen to be one of those people you're talking about."

This always led to great embarrassment on the part of the offender and the apologies would flow rapidly. Sometimes we would just leave. Depending on what part of Atlanta we were in, we often would receive obvious stares. Jim always told me that people were not staring at us, that they were staring at me because I was beautiful. As complimentary and sincere as his explanation was, I knew differently. As progressive as Atlanta was supposed to be, it was the South, and there were still many people there with very prejudiced views.

When you are a minority, you are used to being in situations and circumstances where you are different. So I could always go anywhere and feel comfortable no matter what the racial or ethnic makeup of the crowd was. However, in the early part of our marriage, Jim admitted that he often felt awkward or out of place in situations where he was the only white person because he felt like all eyes were on him and everyone was watching his every move as if they were inspecting him thoroughly. Whenever we would go to a "black event" where dancing was involved, I have to admit that even I would feel a little awkward because, while Jim had great rhythm when it came to playing the piano, he had no rhythm when it came to dancing. He danced very much like a stereotypical white guy! His body seemed jerky, and he danced off beat. He's gotten much better over the years, though.

Being in an interracial marriage, it was very easy for other people to assume that race was the factor if I went to party or an event without Jim. Some people would imply that Jim wasn't there because he didn't want to be with a bunch of black people. But the truth is, if Jim didn't go with me to a social event, it never had anything to do with race. It would just be because of some commonplace, legitimate reason − a business trip, an illness, or some other conflict.

There were some things I had to try to educate Jim about over the years relative to the difference in attitudes between the majority and the minority. For example, he once asked me why black people seem to gravitate and congregate together in a mixed crowd that's predominantly white. I explained to him that it's instinctive for people to gravitate to what they immediately feel comfortable with or feel some identity to. I asked him, "If you were in a crowd with mostly women and only a few men, wouldn't you naturally be inclined to gravitate over to the men?" Whether it's gender or race, it's a natural reaction. Put in that context, he understood my point.

I'll never forget the time he was listening to a black radio talk show, and the discussion was about the Organization of 100 Black Men. He actually called in to the show and commented that he found this organization and its mission very interesting but wondered what would happen if someone started an organization called 100 White Men. The radio talk show host commented, "There's already an organization of 100 white men. It's called the Senate!" Jim laughed and said, "Okay, you got me. There's not much I can say to that." Jim and I did develop our own little private jokes between us over the years. I've always liked my coffee very light with lots of sugar, while he likes his, as he would say, "Black and strong like my woman."

While Jim and I grew up with similar family backgrounds, he has always commented how he admires and envies the closeness and love that is so evident in my family. I definitely grew up in a much more touchy-feely family his. While I grew up with an abundance of unconditional love that was expressed openly, he grew up with love more or less being understood or implied. He has always been very close to his mother, Marilynn, and she is a beautiful person who is very caring. But his relationship with his father up until his death in January 2002 was always a little strained. I consider it a true blessing that during the Christmas we spent with Jim's family prior to his father's sudden death, Jim and his father had a great time together, and his father told him, "I love you," something Jim had not heard in many years.

Right before Jim and I got married, he bought a beautiful six-foot grand piano and decided to have it delivered to my townhouse instead of his house in Albany. He didn't want to have to move it once we got married. The only place it could fit without being in the way was in the dining room. I was very happy when Jim and I bought our first home together, six months after we were married. It was a brand new three-bedroom house, and we finally had a large enough living room with a perfect corner for the piano. Our subdivision comprised mostly young couples around our ages, who either had very young children or were trying to start families. Over the next few months we were consumed with getting comfortable in our new home – decorating, purchasing new furniture, and landscaping our yard. I was so distracted by these activities that getting pregnant was the last thing on my mind. Little did I know that we were about to get a pleasant surprise.

CHAPTER NINE

The Creation of a Miracle

My parents came to visit us four months after we moved into our home, ten months into our marriage. My mother's psychic abilities were confirmed yet again when she informed me that I was pregnant before I had even missed a menstrual cycle. My mom was in the kitchen cooking breakfast for us one morning. I walked into the kitchen and kissed her good morning, and she said, "It is a good morning because you're pregnant."

I laughed and said, "I haven't even missed a period yet."

She said, "But you will because you are definitely pregnant." Well, as usual, she was right. The next week, my monthly visitor failed to appear, and two weeks later my doctor confirmed that I was very much pregnant!

Jim and I and our families were ecstatic about our pregnancy news. While my parents were already blessed to have other grandchildren, this was going to be Jim's parents' first grandchild. From the moment I found out I was pregnant, I began to try to keep my body healthy. I immediately stopped smoking with no problem at all. I tried to eat healthier meals, as I was always sort of a junk-food eater. I glowed with excitement about the thought that Jim and I were going to be parents, but it was also a scary feeling. I wondered how much our lives would change now that we would have this other little helpless miracle who would be totally dependent on us. Jim and I were used to being spontaneous, picking up and going whenever and wherever we wanted to. We lived life by the seat of our pants and somewhat on the edge. I knew that having a child would probably change our level of spontaneity. I also was consumed with thoughts of what our child would look like. Would the baby be healthy? Would it have all of its fingers and toes? I suppose these are normal thoughts that any new mother-to-be has. But the naked truth is that I was also wondering if our child would look black or white or just look like a perfect blend of the two of us.

Within a few weeks of having my pregnancy confirmed by my doctor, the reality hit me very hard when I began feeling extremely nauseous. I didn't just have morning sickness - I had downright misery for the entire first six months of my pregnancy. I was as sick as a dog and couldn't seem to keep any food in my stomach. Even the smell of some foods would make me nauseous. Working became a challenge, as I spent a lot of time in the bathroom throwing up. But my colleagues and customers were very sympathetic and understood when I would abruptly leave a meeting, looking rather green.

On our first wedding anniversary, I was two months pregnant. Jim and I wanted to go out for a romantic dinner to celebrate, but I could only muster the strength to have a romantic split-pea-soup meal in the dining room of our home. I ate crackers constantly to try to keep my stomach settled and to try to ease the nauseating feeling that stuck with me like my new best friend. But I knew that it would all be worth it.

Looking back, I now think that my first daughter was already trying to tell me to get prepared because she would be a hell raiser! She was already showing me that she would do things her way and in her time. As sick as I was in those first two trimesters of pregnancy, I constantly rubbed my small but protruding stomach and talked to my child, telling her how much I loved her. I remember thinking, *even though you're making me feel miserable right now, I'll never stop loving you.* I had no idea that 14 years later I would say those very same words to her.

It didn't matter to Jim or me whether we had a girl or boy. Like most parents, we just wanted to have a healthy baby. But deep within, I sort of knew we were having a girl. I had an ultrasound, and the doctor asked Jim and me if we wanted to know the sex. They couldn't tell definitively from the ultrasound, but they told us they thought it was a girl. I was already visualizing what our little princess would be like. All the little frilly outfits I could dress her in. Perhaps she would take on my love of ballet and become a ballerina. I had all my hopes and dreams of what I wanted for her and what I wanted her to be like. I never gave thought to the reality that this child would be an individual with a mind of her own and her own hopes, dreams, and even failures and pain. I didn't realize then that no matter what we want for our children, they reach a point in life where they make their own choices, good or bad, and we have to suffer the consequences with them as their parents. It's a chilling realization now.

My last trimester of pregnancy was great. I was no longer sick, and I was absolutely glowing. Everyone at work noticed the change in me. I didn't experience any of the swelling in my hands or feet that is so common for many women during the last phase of pregnancy. I only gained 24 pounds and, instead of buying a lot of maternity clothes, I was able to get away with just wearing oversized regular clothes. Jim and I were busy getting the nursery put together and decorated. He painted the top half of the nursery wall pink and put blue pinstriped wallpaper on the bottom half of the wall. It was absolutely beautiful. We set up the crib, changing table, and armoire, and the room was all set for the arrival of our little princess. I would go into the nursery every night, turn the mobile hanging above the crib on, and sit in the rocking chair imagining what it would be like once our little bundle of joy entered this world and would actually be in my arms.

My estimated due date was April 30, but we had been told that first babies usually come later than anticipated. Jim and I attended childbirth classes, and I made the decision that I had no intention of trying to have natural childbirth. I definitely wanted an epidural! In our childbirth classes, they prepared us for the fact that newborn babies usually don't enter this world looking like beautiful little specimens. They told us that often their heads are shaped funny, their skin is blotchy, and sometimes they look downright frightening. They even showed us photographs of newborn babies to help set our expectations properly. So Jim and I were fully prepared that our little princess would most likely enter this world late and may look like less than the perfect little beauty we had imagined.

On April 17, 1988, Jim woke me up to let me know that he was running out to Home Depot to buy more shrubs for the yard. I got out of bed when he left and decided to take a shower and get dressed. I turned on my curling iron, turned the shower on, and just as I was about to set foot in the shower, I got a contraction. It definitely was strong enough to grab my attention, but

I didn't think too much of it since it was two weeks before my actual due date. I proceeded to get in the shower, and, as I lathered up with soap, I got another contraction. Now I was a little concerned because that was two contractions only six or seven minutes apart. I rinsed off hurriedly and got out of the shower, dried off quickly and threw on some sweat pants and a pullover. I started curling my hair and, low and behold, had another strong contraction. There was no doubt in my mind now that I was in labor. I'm not sure, but I think my water must have broken while I was in the shower. I quickly applied a little make-up and actually started to paint my toenails! Okay, the truth is that I've always been a little vain, and I was determined that even if I had to let all dignity go during childbirth, I would at least have pretty feet and freshly painted toes! Just as I was applying polish to the last toe, I got one more strong contraction. I was trying to stay calm and not panic, but I was very worried, as my contractions were now about five minutes apart. I knew that Jim wouldn't be back for about an hour, and I tried to decide what to do.

Amazingly, the phone rang and it was Jim's mom, Marilynn. She just called to see how I was doing. I told her that I thought I was in labor and that Jim was at Home Depot. I also told her that my contractions were only five minutes apart. She told me to try to relax and practice my breathing; she would leave immediately to come get me. Jim's mom lived about 45 minutes away from us. I wasn't sure if she would get to me before Jim, but now I was seriously contemplating calling 911. I went in the living room and squatted on the floor, rocking back and forth, praying to God, *please don't let this baby come while I'm in the house alone.* When Jim's mom arrived, my contractions were about three to four minutes apart, and I had the urge to push. She brought her daughter Cheryl with her. They put me in the front seat of the car, and Cheryl got in the back. Some of our neighbors were outside working in their yards, and Marilynn yelled to them that we were on our way to the hospital and to be on the lookout for Jim. The hospital was a 30-minute drive from our house, and Marilynn drove like a bat out of hell with her flashers on. I kept saying, "I have to push." I had my legs straddled up on the dashboard of the car, and Marilynn and Cheryl both kept saying, "Don't push!"

When we arrived at the hospital, Cheryl ran in and told them, "My sister-in-law is having a baby in the car right now. Come quick." The hospital staff came out to the car, got me on the stretcher, and was pulling my sweats down as they rolled me in. I could feel the pressure of the baby's head, and all I wanted to do was push her out. They got me in the birthing room, and the doctor checked me. I was fully dilated, and he said, "This baby is ready to come out." I was begging for an epidural, and the doctor told me I was so close to delivering that an epidural wasn't necessary. He quickly changed his mind after I became almost hysterical and was upsetting some of the other patients. He gave me the epidural, and I quickly settled down.

Meanwhile, as Jim told me later, he turned into our subdivision about ten minutes after his mom had picked me up. All of our neighbors were trying to flag him down, and he thought they were just waving to him. But he quickly realized they were frantically trying to tell him something, so he rolled down his window and was informed that I was in labor and his mom had left for the hospital with me about ten minutes prior. Jim rushed to the hospital, but he said he kept thinking to himself, *even if Lisa is in labor, it will be many hours before the baby would actually arrive.* After all, in childbirth class, they told us that first labors are generally very long.

Jim arrived at the hospital, and I remember the look he had as if it were yesterday. He was wearing a pink and blue polo shirt and a pair of white slacks. For some reason he reminded me of an ice cream man. He had a look of utter confusion on his face as one of the delivery nurses handed him a pair of scrubs and told him to hurry up and put them on. I was ready to deliver. Up until then, Jim's mom had been in the room with me holding my hand. Every time I would get a sharp contraction, I would grab hold of her and bury my face in her chest. She was wearing a white knit top, and the imprint of my face was left there from my makeup rubbing off. I remember her looking at Jim with a sigh of relief when he walked in. She left the room, and, with three pushes, our baby girl entered this world. Jim cut the umbilical cord, and it was the most magical moment of both of our lives.

After the nurses cleaned the baby up and suctioned out her nose and mouth, they bundled her up and put her in my arms. I took one look at her and immediately noticed that she looked nothing like those photos of newborns that had been shown to us in childbirth class. I know that every new mother thinks her baby is the most beautiful baby in the world, but I have to candidly say that ours really was. She had a perfectly round head, beautiful pinkish olive skin with no blotches, and a full head of straight brown hair. She opened her eyes, and they were a bluish-green color. She immediately reminded me of Jim's grandmother, who had recently passed away. Jim held her briefly, and then the nurse whisked her away to be checked out by the pediatrician. Meanwhile, Jim went out to the waiting room to let his mom and sister know, "It's a girl!"

A day and a half later, Jim and I left the hospital with our new bundle of joy, Kristin Nicole. I actually walked out of the hospital wearing my regular size 4 Calvin Kline jeans, even though they were a little snug. I felt great, and I must admit that I looked great too. My skin was absolutely glowing. No one in the lobby of the hospital could believe that I had given birth in the last 48 hours. Jim pulled the car up to the patient pickup area, and we strapped our little princess into her brand new car seat in the backseat of our car. I got in the front seat on the passenger's side, and, just as we were pulling away, Jim turned on the radio. I felt as if I were in a scene from a movie because the song that was playing could not have been more appropriate. It was Stevie Wonder's "Isn't She Lovely." As Jim and I listened to the song, we were both overcome with emotion and tears streamed down our faces. They were tears of utter happiness. We never could have imagined then that 14 years later we would be crying tears of a different kind over this same little angel.

When we arrived home, I held Kristin in my arms, and Jim and I walked from room to room giving her a tour of her new home. Even though we had set up a bassinette in our bedroom for her to sleep in for the first few weeks of being in this world, I wanted to introduce her to her very own room and crib. I laid Kristin in her crib and turned the mobile on. Again I was overcome with emotion, as I had sat in the rocking chair in her nursery for so many nights while I was pregnant, listening to that mobile playing and fantasizing about what it would be like once she was finally here. I had to pinch myself to be assured that I was not dreaming. Our little creation was really lying there right before my very eyes. She was more beautiful than I could have ever imagined.

Even though Kristin slept through the night her first night home, it was many months later before that ever happened again. It was yet one more validation that everything about our pregnancy and birth experience had gone against the norm – the prolonged morning sickness, her early arrival, the extremely fast labor, and the fact that she had entered this world looking perfect. I suppose I shouldn't have been surprised, though. After all, Jim and I were masters at going against the norm.

Everyone had warned us that our lives would change after having a baby, but it really didn't change our lives that much at all. We just took Kristin everywhere with us and even managed to continue to do things somewhat spontaneously. However, I do recall having to remind Jim on more than one occasion that just picking up and going required a little more work than before we had a baby. As helpful as he was, getting Kristin dressed and packing all the necessities for a baby in tow usually fell on my shoulders.

We adjusted quickly to parenthood and fell into a routine that we all seemed to be comfortable with. Since I was not breastfeeding, Jim and I shared feeding responsibilities fairly equally. He also did his fair share of diaper changing, bathing, dressing, and even getting up with the baby in the middle of the night. Some of my fondest first memories of Jim and Kristin are of him sitting at the piano, playing with one hand as he held her with the other.

After a three-month maternity leave, I returned to work. I actually received a promotion a very short time after returning. This was my first confirmation that IBM had not made an assumption that I was now on the "mommy track" career wise. We had hired the woman who had been our cleaning lady to take care of Kristin in our home, which took a little of the stress off when I went back to work. We didn't have the pressure and stress of the drop-off and pickup routine that many new parents face when dealing with day care. Our childcare giver was wonderful with the baby and took great care of her. Even though her primary responsibilities were caring for

Kristin, I returned home every evening from work to find a spotless house, and she even did the laundry several times a week.

Over the next several months, Jim and I easily settled into parenthood and enjoyed watching Kristin grow. We savored each and every new discovery our little angel made – her first word, her first laugh, the first time she sat up, turned over, and crawled, and, of course, her first steps. Every day, she looked more and more like Jim. People used to comment, and still do, that "she looks like a carbon copy of Jim." My mother told us that we should have named her Jamie after Jim, which is short for James.

We bought another new home when Kristin was six months old. This home was much larger, and we had more room than we knew what to do with. In fact, Jim had surprised me with it. I had flown to Miami with Kristin for Nerissa's wedding. Upon returning to Atlanta, Jim picked us up from the airport. As we approached our neighborhood, Jim turned down a different street. He simply said, "I want to show you something." He turned into a new subdivision under development that had a few completed homes that were all quite large. He pulled in the driveway of a beautiful red brick home and said, "Let's go in and take a look."

Before we even entered the house, I commented, "Wow, this house is huge." We went inside and walked around. I loved the house.

Jim asked, "Do you really like this house?"

I said, "Yes. It's beautiful, and it's so big."

He responded, "Good. I'm glad you like it because I put a contract on it."

A few months later we moved into our second new home. Between working, being parents, and decorating yet another house, we stayed busy. We had absolutely no idea that we were about to get another huge surprise.

CHAPTER TEN

A Big Surprise

Before Jim and I had a baby, one of our favorite places to go was the beach in Destin, Florida. It was about a five-hour drive from Atlanta and a quick little long-weekend getaway. We took Kristin on her first trip to Destin when she was 10 months old. We had a great time and even managed to have some romantic moments, even with baby in tow. In fact, perhaps a little too romantic, as our second child was conceived there and was totally unplanned. She was definitely a "love child."

About a month after our Destin trip, I started feeling very tired and lethargic. I felt a little queasy in the mornings and had a strong sense that I was pregnant, but I was in deep denial and didn't mention anything to Jim. I had to go on a business trip to Boca Raton, Florida, for a few days, and it was going to be Jim's first time staying alone with Kristin for more than a day. When I arrived in Boca, I went to a drug-store and bought two home pregnancy tests. I went back to the hotel and took the first test. The results were positive, and I immediately took the second test almost hoping that I would get a different result, it too was positive however. We had been using the rhythm method for birth-control and it had obviously failed. I did a quick calculation to try to determine how far apart our children would be and estimated that their age difference would be about 18 months. I thought I was going to pass out at this revelation. I couldn't imagine having two babies in diapers. While Jim and I had casually talked about having a second child, we certainly weren't expecting or planning to have one this soon after the first.

I honestly didn't know how Jim was going to take the news, as I was struggling with accepting it myself. I called him to see how he and Kristin were doing. He said, "We're doing great, everything is going fine. We're just sitting here watching TV and having some pizza and beer."

I said, "Are you enjoying fatherhood?"

He replied, "Sure I am. Why?"

I responded, "Because we're going to have another baby. I'm pregnant."

All in one breath he said, "Oh wow. Are you sure? How did that happen?"

I found the "How did that happen" question a little humorous – as if he didn't know how it happened! I told him that I had taken two pregnancy tests, both positive, and that I had been feeling tired and queasy. I said, "Jim, there's no doubt about it. I'm definitely pregnant."

With that, he said, "Okay babe, another baby it is." He told me that he and Kristin missed me and loved me. I told him that I loved and missed them too. We said good night and hung up. I sat on the edge of my hotel bed for the next few minutes trying to convince myself that two babies 18 months apart wouldn't be so hard. But as I would later learn – boy was I wrong.

My second pregnancy was much easier than my first. I had only a short bout of morning sickness and felt great for the duration of my pregnancy. I only gained 26 pounds but showed much sooner than I had the first go round. I actually bought and wore real maternity clothes this time. But I was all stomach. Again, I had none of the usual swelling of my hands or feet. Our families were again very excited about another baby on the way, and I think they were all hoping it would be a boy this time. Jim and I really didn't care if it was a boy or another girl. We just wanted a healthy baby.

My obstetrician had warned me that second labors are usually much faster than the first. Since my first labor was so quick, he told me to get to the hospital the minute I felt a contraction. My estimated due date was October 17, 1989. Since Kristin came two weeks early, I expected that this baby would come a little early as well.

I think subconsciously I was trying to rush Kristin along in her development in anticipation of a new baby coming. I desperately tried to get her potty trained, but to no avail. Jim and I constantly told her that she was going to have a new little brother or sister. I let her feel the baby moving in my stomach. She would often kiss my stomach and say, "Hi baby." We bought her a new, big-girl bed, as we didn't want to buy a second crib. In retrospect, that was a major mistake.

Seeing how this was the last quarter of the year and Jim was a sales rep at IBM, he was very busy trying to get some huge deals closed. He worked long hours and was under a lot of pressure to ensure he would make or exceed his sales quota. In addition, we needed some sizable commission checks to come in to give us a financial cushion, as we now had a larger mortgage and were about to have another mouth to feed. We also decided that, with two babies and my plan to continue to work, we would hire a live-in nanny, which was also going to be an additional major expense.

Having Jim's family living in Atlanta was a godsend. They enjoyed spending time with Kristin, and we counted on them often to keep her overnight when we had weekend plans that weren't conducive to bringing her along. It was perfect timing that our busy little toddler was staying with them the morning I went into labor, October 20, 1989. It was already three days past my due date, and I was awakened by a very sharp contraction. Jim was already dressed and about to leave for work. In fact, he had a big meeting with a client – the deal of his life hanging by a thread. I told him, "I'm in labor; we need to go the hospital now." He gave me a look that showed me he was thinking, *this is not good timing.* He made a quick phone call to his client to let them know that he was on his way to the hospital because I was in labor. We gathered up my things and left for the hospital.

We arrived at the hospital, and the doctor examined me. As it turned out, I was only dilated a few centimeters, and, if it had not been for my previous labor history, they would have sent me back home. Instead, they had me walk around for a while and then sit in a whirlpool bath. After several hours, I still was not progressing much further along in labor. They finally gave me an epidural, induced labor, and hooked me up to a monitor. They showed Jim how to watch the monitor to determine when a contraction was occurring. Unlike my first pregnancy, I felt no pain.

We were in a birthing room that looked very much like a bedroom in a home. Jim sat in a chair next to the bed and was on the phone with his client trying to get his deal closed. Every once in a while he would say to his client, "Hang on a second, Lisa's having another contraction." He would talk me through my breathing, and when the contraction ended, he would go back to his phone conversation. I had met his client before, and we had actually had dinner with him and his wife several times. So his client was actually excited that, in a weird way, he was going through this experience with us!

After 14 hours of labor, I was finally ready to deliver. Unlike baby one, baby two had decided to take its own sweet time in making its entrance into this world. The delivery went flawlessly, and as soon as the baby was out, Jim and the doctor said almost in unison, "It's a girl." I was actually excited that it was another girl. Jim, like before, cut the umbilical cord. The nurse took the baby and did the usual quick cleanup and suctioning and put the baby in my arms. But right away, I noticed this baby looked very different than Kristin did when she was born. Her head was shaped funny, her skin was blotchy, and the naked truth is she looked very much like those newborn photos we had seen in childbirth class. She looked a little frightening. Nevertheless, Jim and I ogled and awed over her for a few minutes, and then she was whisked away to be examined by the pediatrician.

Once I was moved to my room, Jim asked me in a very concerned manner, "The baby looks funny to me. Do you think there's something wrong with her?" I assured him that the baby was fine, that she just looked like most newborns look. After about an hour, they brought the baby in the room and told us that she was healthy. She looked a lot better than she did upon entering the world, but she still didn't have that perfect look of beauty that we had experienced with our first child. Her coloring was much better, but her skin tone was very yellow and it was later determined she was a little jaundiced. She had a full head of straight black hair, and her bangs were so long they came down almost to her eyes. She looked very much like an Eskimo. We named her Jennifer Ryan.

Jim and I had already decided that we did not want to have a third child. He was very adamant that it was fine with him that he did not have a son. He didn't want to risk going for a boy because, with our luck, we might end up with twins and two more girls! We had already arranged with my doctor to have my tubes tied, and it was to be done the day after Jennifer's arrival. I was 29 years old, and I was quite content with having two children. I felt very comfortable with our decision to have no more and ensure that there would be no accidents with a fairly permanent method of birth control.

The day before I was released from the hospital, Jim came in my hospital room and said, "I have a surprise for you."

He handed me a car key, and I asked, "What's this?"

He said, "Now, with two car seats and two babies, I thought a bigger four-door car made more sense."

He had bought me a brand new Jeep Cherokee so I wouldn't have to drive my two-door BMW when carting the kids around. I had constantly complained about the difficulty of getting Kristin in the backseat and strapping her into her car seat. I was so happy and impressed that somehow he had managed to find the time to go buy a new car for me in the midst of everything else that was going on. He had closed the deal with his client, so he was clearly flying on cloud nine.

The day we left the hospital to bring Jennifer, our latest little addition, home, I wasn't feeling or looking as good as I did when we went through the same routine 18 months before. I was very sore and had a lot of cramping as a result of the tube-tying surgery. While I did manage to squeeze into my regular size 4 jeans, I could zip them only halfway up and had to wear a long sweatshirt over them. This time, it was fairly obvious that I had just given birth. Kristin had already been introduced to her new baby sister, as Jim had brought her to the hospital to visit the day after Jennifer was born. I fondly remember Kristin sitting in the chair in my hospital room eating an apple as Jim and I tried to show her the new baby. She seemed so unaffected by it all. I'm not sure that her little mind really comprehended that this baby was coming home with us and staying. I'm not sure she understood that all the love, affection, and attention that were showered on her would now have to be shared with Jennifer, this new little creation.

When we were all strapped in our new Jeep Cherokee and pulled away from the patient pickup area, Jim turned on the radio like he did before. But I honestly don't even remember what was playing. Whatever it was, it wasn't anything emotionally moving. The drive home was very peaceful, as both baby and toddler slept. I remember thinking, *this is all going to be okay*. But it would take less than 24 hours for me to think differently.

CHAPTER ELEVEN

Entering the Super Mom Zone

Although Jim and I had settled into parenthood with no problems after our first child, it was clear that life would be much more difficult with the addition of this second little bundle of joy. From the time we brought Jennifer home, it was evident that she was going to be a difficult baby. As much as our lives hadn't changed that much after Kristin, life changed drastically with the addition of Jennifer.

Jennifer cried and screamed all the time. She was very colicky, and it was frustrating that nothing seemed to make her comfortable. She slept for only two hours at a time, which meant that no one else in the house slept either. We were all sleep-deprived and cranky.

My mom flew in from Miami to stay with us for a few weeks to help out after Jennifer was born. She immediately could tell that I was frazzled. Kristin had suddenly become very whiny and actually started regressing. The combination of a whiny toddler and a screaming baby kept me on edge.

Everybody and everything got on my nerves. My mom had me try all the old-fashioned remedies to settle a colicky baby, but none of them seemed to work. So, she resorted to the one thing she had done all her life – she prayed over the baby and even anointed her head with oil. Miraculously, Jennifer seemed to settle down somewhat.

After a couple of weeks, my mom had to get back to Miami. The day she left, I cried and told her that I didn't think I could do this. She assured me that I was going to be just fine. I really had come to understand how some mothers end up hurting or even unintentionally killing their babies. While there was no way I would ever do anything intentionally to harm either one of my children, I could certainly rationalize how and why it happens sometimes. When you are suffering from sleep depravation and you constantly have a screaming baby, it's very easy to just snap. Without any help or a strong support system, I really believe that some women go temporarily insane and do things that they normally would not even think about doing when they're in their right frame of mind. But let me be clear – I am not giving justification to anyone harming her child; it's totally unacceptable and intolerable. But I do have some degree of empathy when I hear about it happening, particularly with young, single mothers with no support system.

I vividly remember an incident that I think scared Jim out of his wits. Jennifer was screaming one night, and I told Jim, "I can't get up; you have to get up with her."

He replied, "Lisa, I have to try to get some sleep. I have to get up and go to work in a few hours."

I said, "If I get up and get that baby, I think I'm going to throw her over the banister of the stairs." I jumped out of bed and stormed into the nursery. Before I knew it, Jim ran past me and whisked Jennifer out of her crib. He held her tight in his arms and looked at me with great concern. He asked, "You wouldn't actually throw her over the banister, would you?" I started crying and, between my sobs, responded, "Of course not. I'm just so tired and feel like I'm a complete failure at being a good mom." With that, I took the baby from him. I changed her diaper, and Jim went downstairs to warm her bottle. He came back upstairs and handed me her bottle. I then sat in the rocking chair and gave her the bottle. As I rocked her, she screamed and I cried. Jim knelt beside us and tried to comfort us both. She finally went to sleep. Jim and I got back into bed, and he held me in his arms as he stroked my back and very softly said, "Lisa, everything is going to be okay. I love you. Let's get some sleep."

A few days after that incident, Jim's mom called him and suggested we let her take the kids for a few days so I could get some rest. Jim said, "I don't think Lisa will let the baby stay overnight this soon." She said, "Trust me. She will." Even though Jennifer was only four weeks old, I was more than willing to let Marilynn keep her and Kristin for a few days. I knew I could use some down time and the rest. We drove to Jim's parents' house with both kids in tow. His mom had actually turned one of the extra bedrooms in their home into a nursery after Kristin was born, so she had a complete baby setup.

We arrived at Jim's parents' home and visited for a while. Ironically, up until this point, I had never viewed Jim's father as a warm and fuzzy person. However, he was the one person who could hold Jennifer and seem to keep her quiet. It melted my heart to see this man who I had viewed as sort of cold sitting in his big chair ogling over this baby and showing her genuine love. I knew that Jim's father had great concern for our children and how they would be viewed or accepted in society as a product of a mixed-race marriage. But it was so obvious that he loved his grandkids, and he worried about seeing their hearts get broken. I think that was the day I found a special place in my heart for Jim's father. As mentioned previously, Jim always had sort of a strained relationship with his father. But for some reason, I felt this special connection with his father that I can't explain. It's as if we sort of silently understood each other. I had grown to love my father-in-law, and I was very sad at his sudden death in January of 2002.

Those few days that Jim's parents kept our children were exactly what I needed. What we needed. I think I slept more than I had slept in four weeks. It gave me a chance to reflect and get a grip on reality. I was now the mother of two very young children who needed me. This was no time for me to become a weakling. They needed me to be strong and healthy, physically and mentally. I stopped feeling sorry for myself and counted my blessings that I had a wonderful husband who was very helpful, as well as a vast array of family and close friends as a support system. I knew I had to pull it all together, as I was returning to work in January right after the New Year.

Those next few weeks after my little break from the kids were much better. Even though Jennifer still cried and screamed frequently and Kristin whined constantly, I handled it much better. Jennifer started to sleep for longer periods of time, and I adjusted much better to our new schedule. Kristin finally got the hang of potty training, and she even stayed in her big-girl bed through the night versus climbing out and getting in the bed with Jim and me. When Jennifer would scream in the middle of the night, Kristin would sleep through it as if she had learned to tune it out. It seemed as if we were all finally getting into a rhythm and things were going much smoother. But the naked truth is that Jim and I both seemed to be having a hard time bonding with this new baby. But something happened that changed that forever.

Jennifer was six weeks old, and Kristin was a year and a half. Kristin had a cold, and a few days later it seemed that Jennifer had what I thought was just a cold too. Jim and I had plans to go out one night, and his sister, Cheryl, came over to baby sit. When Jim and I returned home around midnight, Cheryl told us that both of the kids were fine and asleep but that the baby seemed really congested. I said goodnight to Cheryl as she was leaving, and I went upstairs to check on the kids. When I looked in on Jennifer, her coloring looked funny to me, and she seemed to be struggling to breathe. I immediately screamed for Jim to come upstairs. I told him, "I think this baby is really sick. I should take her to the hospital."

Jim said, "Lisa, she just has a cold. She'll be alright. Just take her to the pediatrician tomorrow."

But I followed my maternal instincts and said, "No, something is really wrong with her. I'm taking her to the hospital NOW."

He said, "Okay, take her if that will make you feel better. I'll stay here with Kristin."

I bundled Jennifer up to brave the cold outside. I strapped her in her car seat and dashed off for the emergency room. By the time I reached the emergency room, it was very obvious to me that Jennifer was really struggling to breathe. I literally ran into the emergency room with her in my arms. The triage nurse took one look at her and said, "Follow me." She got us into a room, and within a few seconds, the resident pediatrician came in. He listened to her chest and asked, "How long has this baby been sick?"

I responded, "She's had a cold for a couple of days."

He looked at me almost with disgust and said, "Ma'am, your baby doesn't have a cold. She has pneumonia. Her lungs are full of fluid. She's very sick, and we need to admit her to the hospital."

With that, I began sobbing uncontrollably. But this pediatrician showed me no sympathy; he went on to say, "Had you not brought her to the emergency room, she probably would have died during the night." Before I knew it, there was a cascade of hospital folks in the room. One person placed an oxygen mask over my baby's tiny face, while another one drew blood, and another tried to get an IV line started.

I was crying hysterically and couldn't bear to watch all the pricking and prodding that was occurring to my six-week-old baby. One of the nurses tried to comfort me and told me that it might be easier if I stepped out the room for a few minutes. I asked to use the phone so I could call Jim. The phone rang once and he picked it up. He heard me sobbing and said, "Oh my God Lisa. What's going on?" Between my sobs I managed to tell him that our baby had pneumonia and was very sick and that they were admitting her to the hospital. I then said almost in an angry tone, "Jim, she probably would have died had I not brought her to the hospital." I have no recollection of what he said back to me, but I do remember hanging up the phone. I may have actually hung up on him. I went back into the room, and they were ready to take Jennifer to her hospital room. She had all sorts of things hooked up to her. They had her in a small crib with an oxygen tent over it.

By now, it was about 2:00 in the morning, and I was running on pure adrenaline. As I was about to step into the elevator with the hospital staff who was taking Jennifer to her room, the pediatrician who had made me feel like the worst mother in the world walked up to me and gently touched my arm. He said, "Your baby is very sick, but I think she's going to be okay." I could only manage to nod my head as the tears streamed down my face. Once Jennifer and I were both in her room, the nurse got a blanket for me and told me the chair in the room fully reclined, so I should be able to get some sleep. But I couldn't think about sleep, and I wouldn't dare close my eyes while my baby struggled for her life. The nurse left the room. As I stood over the crib and looked at Jennifer through that oxygen tent, I resorted to that solid foundation of prayer that I had grown up with. I prayed out loud, "God, please don't take my baby from me. Please make her well. God, if you heal this baby, I will never, ever complain about her again. I promise you that her screams and cries will be a joyful noise unto the Lord. I'm putting all my trust in you and leaving her in your hands. Please just heal her, God."

Then I called my mother. I'm sure the phone ringing in the middle of the night startled her, but hearing my voice totally alarmed her. I told her what had happened, and she prayed with me there on the phone as she had done so many other times in my life. She told me that she was going to call her prayer chain immediately. She said, "Lisa, I know you believe in the power of prayer. Don't lose your faith. God will heal this baby." I hung up the phone, went back over to the crib, and stood there all night reciting the Lord's Prayer over and over again.

God answered our prayers. Two and a half days later, Jim and I brought Jennifer home. I kept my promise to God and never complained about her again, and neither did Jim. She still cried and screamed a lot, but it had become almost like music to our ears. From that day forward, any time either one of our kids had so much as a cough, we headed to the doctor's office or the hospital. I never again allowed Jim or myself to try to make our own medical diagnosis and risk either one of our children's lives. I think our pediatrician actually got tired of seeing me and my kids in his office for every little cough or sneeze. But it didn't matter to me. I definitely used the "better safe than sorry" rationalization.

My first big venture out alone with Jennifer and Kristin was a trip to the mall. It was a few weeks before Christmas, and I was way behind in my Christmas shopping. It was the middle of the week, and I thought I would get the kids dressed, fed, and out of the house so we could arrive at the mall just as it was opening – hopefully before it got crowded. We had a double stroller so that Jennifer and Kristin could be pushed easily. Thankfully, both kids fell asleep on the drive to the mall and even managed to stay asleep as I put them in the stroller. I was like a mad woman dashing in and out of stores, buying gifts for family and trying to get as much done before the kids woke up. I accumulated many bags with my purchases and tried to juggle and balance packages, a diaper bag, and a bulky double stroller. I had one more store I needed to go to, and it was on the opposite side of the mall from where I was. As I made my way through what now had become a crowded mall, Jennifer woke up and started crying.

I looked around to see if there was a bench so I could sit and feed her, but there was not a bench anywhere in my vicinity. I tried to push the stroller off to the side to get out of people's way. As I tried to get her bottle out of the diaper bag, she began screaming. Her high-pitched screams woke Kristin up, and then she too screamed. Kristin wanted out of the stroller and wanted me to pick her up. I kept telling her, "Just a minute, sweetie. Mommy has to feed the baby." But she would have none of that "just a minute, sweetie" stuff. She wanted out, and she wanted out now! As I fumbled with the bottle and tried to pick the baby up out of the stroller,

Kristin proceeded to flail her body around in the stroller and actually tried to climb out, even though she was very tightly strapped in. She started screaming at the top of her lungs, "Pick up! Pick up!" It seemed like every pair of eyes in the mall was on me. I was afraid that Kristin was going to make the stroller tip over. I finally had the baby in my arms and gave her the bottle, holding it under my chin. I used my other hand to try to unstrap Kristin and get her out of the stroller. She then was out of the stroller with her arms raised up in the air still screaming, "Pick up! Pick up!" I said, "Mommy will pick you up in a minute."

I tried to hold her hand while I still had Jennifer in my other arm with the bottle in her mouth, holding the bottle under my chin. Kristin pulled away from my grip, the bottle fell from under my chin, and Kristin threw herself on the ground and flew into a full-fledged temper tantrum. I quickly laid the baby in the stroller, and she started screaming again, as I had clearly interrupted her feeding. I tried to stay calm, but I couldn't fight back the tears. There I was in the middle of a crowded mall, two weeks before Christmas, with one child flailing on the ground screaming, another one in the stroller wailing, and everyone staring at me with either sympathy or disdain.

Well, my "most people really are good people" philosophy proved itself to be true. A very nice older woman came up to me and said, "Honey, if it's okay, I'll help you." Before I could even respond, she picked the baby's bottle up off the ground, wiped the nipple off, knelt by the stroller, and held the bottle in Jennifer's mouth. I picked Kristin up off the ground and held her in my arms; she put her head on my shoulder and whimpered, "Juice, mommy. Juice." I reached in the diaper bag and pulled her juice box out and gave it to her. I stood there rocking her for a few minutes as the nice woman who had come to my rescue continued to hold the bottle for

Jennifer. I put Kristin back in the stroller, and the woman said, "She's done with her bottle. Would you like me to burp her?"

I said, "That's okay. I'll burp her, but thank you so much for your help."

She said, "You're very welcome. I too was a young mother at one time with two very young children close in age."

I picked Jennifer up and burped her, and when I placed her back in the stroller, the nice woman was gone. Both children were quiet, satisfied, and happy. I left the mall immediately and never made it to that last store I was trying to get to. I don't know who the nice woman was or even her name. But whoever and wherever you are, you have no idea how much I appreciated what you did for me that December day in 1989.

I returned to work at the beginning of January, and Jennifer still was not sleeping through the night yet. Our new live in nanny had moved in with us right after Christmas. We found her through the Nanny Institute of Beverly Hills Atlanta campus. We interviewed many candidates and initially were looking for an older nanny. But the one we ended up hiring seemed to fit in with our lifestyle and personalities the best, so we hired her even though she was only 23 years old. I had a few weeks at home with the new nanny before returning to work, so I could show her the kids' routine and observe how she handled them. Initially, it appeared that this nanny arrangement was going to work out well, but I would later learn that I had been overly optimistic.

Just like before, I received a promotion very soon after returning from maternity leave. This was actually a big promotion, as it was my very first management job. Again, I was thrilled and impressed that my maternity leaves didn't seem to have any negative effect on IBM's perception of my career potential. The company clearly assessed my ability and my track record and made no assumptions just because I now had two children 18 months apart. I actually started to wonder about this mommy track that I had read so much about and had heard other new mothers talk about. If it really existed, I hadn't experienced it yet.

Within just a few short months of returning to work, it was quite evident to me that I had entered the Super Mom zone. That "I have to be perfect" syndrome that I had grown up believing started to take its toll. I was trying to be a perfect wife, a perfect mother, a perfect manager, a perfect employee, and a perfect daughter. I wanted to have a perfectly clean and tidy house, even amid the many toys and paraphernalia of two young children. I've always been a romantic, and, as tired as I was at night, I was still passionate and intimate with my husband to ensure we didn't let the fire die in our love life. I even occasionally surprised him by wearing some new little sexy and sometimes uncomfortable lingerie to bed, even though I usually preferred to sleep in his tee shirts. I tried to meet everyone's needs, including my own. I was actually handling it all fairly well, but there's no mistaking that I was stressed out.

Then, as if I didn't already have enough to keep me busy, I enrolled in a jazz dance class that I attended two nights a week! For me, dancing was my way of relieving stress. My dance class was my time for me. I would lose myself in the sound of the music and movement of my body. I pushed myself hard in dance class and often fantasized that I was on Broadway. Even though this was an adult jazz class, most of the participants were in their early 20s, and I was now 30. But I felt just as young as they were and could move just as well, and it made me feel very much alive.

Honestly, the naked truth is that I really did feel as if I could run into a phone booth and change out of my business suit into a spandex jumpsuit with a big "S" on my chest, for I truly believed that I *was* Super Mom!

I don't think Kristin will ever suffer from the Super Mom syndrome. After watching me all these years, she's made it very clear that when she gets married and has kids some day, she wants to be home with her children and raise them herself.

CHAPTER TWELVE

Climbing the Corporate Ladder
before Going Downhill

When I joined IBM in February of 1982, never in my wildest dreams did I imagine that I would have stayed with the company for 22 years or that I would obtain the level of vice president. While many people start out in their careers with high ambitions, it was just a job to me at first. Actually, I thought I would stay with IBM for a few years and then follow my dream of going on to law school. I even had some wild fantasies about trying my luck on Broadway as a dancer or perhaps venturing into the world of modeling or acting full-time. But whenever I would contemplate leaving IBM, it never seemed like the right time. Either I would be in a new job that I loved or I would be learning something new and fascinating that kept my attention. I can certainly say I have never been bored at IBM.

As I reflect back on my career, it's ironic that much of my climbing the corporate ladder happened somewhat accidentally. At times, it felt more like an escalator ride, as I had so many people pulling me along, and I was going along for the ride. My first permanent job with IBM was as a programmer, even though my interest was in sales and marketing. My first year as a programmer was exciting because I had a huge learning curve, and I was like a kid in a video arcade trying to master the secrets of winning the game. I liked programming, but it didn't take me long to realize that I was never going to be passionate about it. After one year, I received my first promotion to associate programmer. One year was the average length of time it took to reach that level, so it was no great accomplishment as far as I was concerned.

As a JES 3 Level 2 programmer, my job was to talk on the phone all day to customers who had a software problem. By the time the problem reached Level 2, it usually meant that it was fairly significant, and often the customer's system was down. This meant that I was talking to unhappy customers who were anxious to have their problems resolved. It was a stressful job, and I often felt like I was in a game of beat the clock. I sat in my own small office with no windows. You could smoke in buildings back in those days, and most of the programmers I worked with were heavy smokers. Even though I had been more of a social smoker back then, I started practically chain-smoking. I remember sitting in my office wearing a telephone headset, listening to less-than-happy customers vent, as I poured through software dumps trying to determine where the software bug was and writing code to get around it. A big white cloud of smoke would circle above me, and an ashtray would be filled with cigarette butts by the end of the day. I've always been a people person, but I like to see people and interact with them, not just talk to them on the phone. Deep in my heart I knew that this programming job was not my cup of tea, and, by year two, I gave serious thoughts to leaving IBM or trying to figure out how to tell my manager that I wanted to do something different.

As devastated as I was at having my first marriage end, it actually was a blessing in disguise from a career standpoint. The opportunity to move to Atlanta and pursue my real interest – sales and marketing – was the silver lining in the dark and gloomy cloud. I absolutely loved my job as a systems engineer. It was challenging, interesting, and fun. I enjoyed spending time with customers and helping them come up with solutions to solve their business problems. I felt a great sense of satisfaction and fulfillment from my work. My customers liked me, trusted me, and respected me. I woke up each morning excited about going to work. It didn't really feel like work to me. The IBM Atlanta Branch office almost felt like family.

I progressed through the SE ranks and received several promotions, but again at average pace by my own standards. However, during a career discussion with my manager one day, he told me that I had the potential to be a manager and eventually an executive. He informed me that he was putting me in Executive Resources, without fully explaining what that meant. I later learned that people on the Executive Resources list were those identified as high-potential candidates, with the ability or potential to be future leaders in IBM. Back then, Executive Resources was like some big secret list. No one talked openly about it. You knew if you were on it, but that's about all you knew. The intent was to ensure that Executive Resources candidates had a development plan in place with specific projects or opportunities, including target dates that would afford them the opportunity to develop concrete skills and career growth, as well as become more competitive for leadership positions. Of course, in later years, Executive Resources became much more openly talked about and

111

understood. It's a fairly formal process, and I can attest to the fact that it works.

About two months after returning to work after my first maternity leave, I received a promotion, which was an opportunity to work in the Atlanta Customer Center and gain experience in marketing. I was really excited about this, as I always viewed myself as a creative person. My responsibilities included developing marketing collateral for some of our key products, developing customer seminars and executive customer briefings, and coordinating customer events around product announcements. I enjoyed this new opportunity and quickly became fascinated with the world of marketing.

I had only been in this new assignment for five months when I learned that I was pregnant with our second child. I wanted to keep my pregnancy hidden for as long as possible because I was unsure how management would view me. While I still wasn't that ambitious as far as my career went, I enjoyed my work and was at least curious about whether or not I could really become a manager. While I was thrilled that my first maternity leave didn't seem to affect my ability to receive a promotion, I was unsure if being pregnant again so soon after the first time would take me out of the running or consideration for a management position.

One of my biggest assignments while in the Customer Center was my responsibility for coordinating a major customer event around the announcement of our RS6000 product. This was a significant product announcement, and we planned a rather large customer event around it. My manager informed me that there was a meeting scheduled to brief one of our high-level executives on our announcement plans. He told me that he wanted me to make the presentation. I was very excited, as this was going to be my first time presenting in front of a key IBM executive. I wasn't nervous because I had always been very comfortable speaking and presenting. I suppose I've always been a bit of a ham and perhaps, subconsciously, I think speaking or presenting in front of an audience is probably the closest I'll ever get to my Broadway fantasy.

I prepared my presentation and reviewed it several times with my manager. On the day of the meeting, I took great care to ensure that I wore my most conservative suit and pulled my hair back in a bun. Although I had become known for being a flamboyant and fashionable dresser, I wanted to look extremely professional that day.

My manager kicked off the meeting by making a short introduction. I then went up to start my presentation, and, before I said a word, the executive said, "So, sweetheart, tell me about this product launch." I immediately felt all the blood drain from my face, as the "sweetheart" comment definitely caught me off guard. I wasn't insulted or offended by the comment because you would have to know this executive to understand that this was just his way, even though it may have been inappropriate, particularly by today's standards. But this was the late '80s, and in the South, women often were still referred to as sweetheart, darling, or honey, even in business settings. I took a deep breath after his comment and launched into my presentation. Even though the executive looked down at the pad of paper in front of him and doodled for much of my presentation, I knew he was listening because he asked me several detailed questions, which I was able to answer. After my presentation, I was supposed to leave the meeting because my manager and the executive had other business to discuss that didn't involve me. As I walked out of the conference room, the executive shook my hand and said, "You did a very nice job." I glanced down to the pad of paper he had been doodling on and noticed that there were little flowers drawn all over the page. I walked out of the room and tried to figure out the meaning behind the flowers he had drawn. Even though I was pregnant, I wasn't showing, and I had not told anyone yet. Yet I couldn't help but think that maybe this was his view of me, that I was a young blossoming flower! Perhaps the flowers had no meaning at all relative to me. But it sure made me perplexed for a few days afterward.

Oddly enough, this executive became a great supporter of mine in later years and even helped me sort through some major career decisions. I never had the courage to ask him if he remembered the flowers. He has since retired from IBM, but perhaps I'll run into him some time in the future and finally ask him if he even remembers the incident and can tell me what on earth those flowers meant!

I mentioned earlier that, very shortly after returning to work from my second maternity leave, I was promoted to my first management job. I considered this a huge leap of faith and confidence in me on the part of the branch manager, George Gagel, and the branch office support manager, Doug Niman, who both interviewed me and made the decision that I was the best candidate for the job. I was very determined to prove to them and everyone else that they had made the right decision. There were even a few folks who jokingly commented to me that I must be out of my mind to take a management job with a newborn baby and a young toddler at home. Honestly, I was a little worried myself and wondered if I was I doing the right thing.

It took me only a few months to get adjusted to intertwining the demands of all these new roles in my life. Back then, I was focused on trying to achieve *balance* between work and life. I later changed my philosophy to reflect the idea that finding *harmony* as opposed to *balance* might be a more realistic objective. That feeling of not wa disappoint anyone or let anyone down was ever present. I felt like it wasn't good enough for me to just meet people's expectations from a professional or personal standpoint - I felt a need to exceed them. It was the beginning of this invariable self-imposed pressure that I put on myself and carried around for numerous years in every facet of my life that ultimately led to complete burnout.

Nevertheless, leadership became intoxicating to me. I loved managing and leading people. In fact, I loved managing *anything*. I enjoyed facilitating change. My previous ambiguous attitude regarding my career suddenly shifted to a higher level of ambition. But at this point, it was still a very cautious shift.

My first management job was as a systems engineer manager of MVS (multiple virtual storage) and storage specialists. I had a team of mostly white males who had all been with IBM a long time and were much older than me. They were all very skilled and technical and were highly respected in their areas of expertise. I was very nervous about how these men would accept having this young, black, and new female manager. I knew that my first few weeks in the job would be critical, as my credibility would be tested. While everyone on my team was great when it came to resolving technical issues, I quickly realized that many of them were lacking in interpersonal skills. I knew this was my strength. I was a master at dealing with people inside IBM, as well as with customers. I was very good at problem solving, and I knew how to get things done with positive results. Within a couple of months in my new role, I started hearing very positive feedback from my team and my management. Every member on my team would tell me, "Lisa, you're the best manager I've ever had." It would become a theme that I would continue to hear throughout my IBM career.

As I got to know many of my team members on a personal level, I often asked them why they thought I was a good manager. After all, I was not an easy manager. I expected a lot from my people, and I drove and pushed them hard. I often challenged their way of thinking, as many of them had a very binary way of looking at situations. But I consistently heard, "You care about your people. You go to bat for us. You make us feel valued and appreciated. And you make our job fun." Their view of me was accurate, for I did care about each and every one of them, and I took their career goals and ambitions personally, as if they were my own. I got great satisfaction out of watching and sharing in their success. I cared about their personal lives, too. We worked very hard, but I made sure that we occasionally took the time to play hard too and have a little fun. I have always believed that people are the greatest asset of any company, and I did my best to ensure that my people knew how much they were valued and appreciated.

In some ways, I think that my being married to a white male helped me somewhat in managing and working with white men. I had sort of an intimate perspective on how white men think. I am certainly not naïve enough to believe or suggest that my husband's views on things are representative of all white men. After all, he married a black woman. But it is definitely a personal and intimate perspective that helped me as a black woman in corporate America deal with white men.

In that first year of my management job, things in my personal life were going quite well. Jennifer suddenly changed and became a very sweet, easy-going child. Kristin started to talk quite well, and it was already apparent to me that she was becoming increasingly precocious. Unfortunately, our live-in nanny arrangement did not work out, and we ended up firing her. The demands of caring for a baby and a toddler were more than she could handle. Not to mention, a few incidents occurred that caused Jim and I to seriously question her character. It was as if the person who had come to live with us to care for our children was a person completely different from the one we had interviewed. The woman who had cared for our first child came back to help us out for a few months while we scrambled to find another nanny. Even though we were originally looking for another live-in nanny, we decided that a live-out nanny would be acceptable, but we definitely wanted someone who could care for our children in our home and could be flexible in the hours she worked. We were blessed to find a young mother who had a son a year older than Kristin. It was the perfect solution for us and for her. She would bring her son with her when she came to our home to care for our children. It gave Kristin a playmate, and the two children got along very well. The nanny was great with our kids, and it was a magnificent arrangement that we kept for over a year.

While I loved my job and had become completely enamored with IBM, Jim became interested in doing something else. I had become quite good at dealing with corporate politics, but Jim had this entrepreneurial spirit about him and was interested in starting his own business. He would often tell me, "You'll go far with IBM. Everyone loves you and thinks that you walk on water, but I want to run my own business." Jim had excellent technical and sales skills, and he was very business savvy. Intuitively, I knew that he would eventually attempt his own start-up.

After about a year and a half in my management job, IBM began making the shift into the Professional Services business, now known as IBM Global Services. This was a major cultural change for our systems engineers because now they were to become billable resources. The work they had been accustomed to doing for *free* was now to be done for *fee*. A Services organization was created, and my organization was to be a part of it. I now was responsible for managing technical specialists for large systems, storage, and printers. My job was to lead these specialists in making the transition to being billable resources. It was a fundamental change to how they were accustomed to operating. It became quite evident that it was not going to be an easy task. People naturally resist change, and my team was no different. I knew that a few of them would not be able to make the transformation, and I would need to either help find another opportunity for them or manage them out of the business. In the end, I had to do a little of both.

Meanwhile, Jim resigned from IBM and followed through with his vision, launching his own market research business. After almost two years in the Services organization, my manager and I agreed that that my next job should be a staff assignment. Back in those days of IBM, it was fairly common to take a staff job after being in management for a few years before moving to a higher level of management. There was an opportunity to work on the Georgia Trading Area Staff in Opportunity Management. We were about to deploy a new opportunity management process and a new tool for the field called OMSY. We also were deploying a new time tracking tool called BART. We knew that my technical background would come in handy for this job, as well as my ability to facilitate and manage change. We had a new Georgia Trading Area general manager, Harris Warsaw, and while I didn't report directly to him, my job necessitated direct interaction with him.

I took the job and initially worked for a woman, Carol Manning. She and I knew each other well, as we had worked together off and on throughout the years. I had a great deal of respect for her as a manager and as a person. We operated more like peers and worked as a team. We had a difficult job, as the field was not excited about this new process and having to enter their sales opportunities into the new tool and account for their time. I knew that some people secretly started referring to me as "The OMSYS Queen."

As difficult as the job was, I was able to do all the things I needed to do to get it done successfully. Jim's business was going well, but he traveled frequently. When he was in town, he worked almost around the clock – not an uncommon practice when you're running your own business. Our kids were now three and four, and I had a severe case of working mother's guilt. I felt that I wasn't spending enough time with my kids, as they were often in bed very soon after I arrived home from work. I felt that I was missing some critical moments in their young lives. While women in the workplace had become quite common, most of the women in our subdivision were stay-at-home moms. Our next-door neighbor was a stay-at-home mom with three young kids. She and I would often talk on the weekends as our kids played together. She would tell me how much she envied me and this great career I had. I in turn would tell her how much I envied her and the fact that she could spend so much time with her kids. We both realized that the grass always looks greener on the other side.

This was the point in my career when Lou Gerstner had come in as IBM's chairman and CEO. IBM was going through some radical changes from a business perspective and from a corporate culture standpoint. The company began to drastically downsize or, perhaps better said, rightsize. Several financial packages were available for people to volunteer to leave the company. But it was only available to individuals whom management deemed as not having skills critical for the business. Jim and I had several discussions about my volunteering to leave IBM. Since his business was going well, we decided that this might be a good time for me to exit IBM and be a stay-at-home mom.

I had a discussion with my manager, Carol, and subsequently with Harris. He informed me that I was not eligible for the package because I was deemed to have critical skills. He told me, "We don't want to lose you, and there's no way we are going to pay you to leave." While I was flattered, I was also angry. I told him that with a three and a four year old at home, I was really struggling with balancing life and work, and I really needed to spend more time with my kids. Harris and I knew each other well at this point on a professional and a personal level. He asked me, "Do you think you would really be happy as a stay-at-home mom?" I responded, "I'm really not sure, but I know I need to do something different." He suggested that we think about other alternatives, such as my working part-time.

After fuming for a few days at not being eligible to take the volunteer package, I began giving some serious thought to the question Harris had so boldly asked me. I really wasn't sure if I would be happy or be totally fulfilled as a stay-at-home mom. The part-time option seemed like it might be a good alternative. However, I felt strongly that even if I were working part-time and receiving part-time pay, I would retain my full-time work ethic because of how I am and how I operate. I started thinking about the job I was doing and dissected exactly how I spent my time every day. It became apparent to me that this was a job that did not require me to be in the office every day. Most of my interactions with people were by the phone. I spent much of my time on the system, running and analyzing various opportunity reports. I came up with a work alternative to discuss with Harris. I wanted to work from home two days a week, on Mondays and Fridays, and come into the office the other three days. This was before telecommuting or working from home was in vogue, so this alternative was definitely thinking outside the box and going against the norm. But like so many things in my life, going against the norm was normal for me!

I met with Harris and presented him with my work alternative proposal. He was a little skeptical at first. But I asked him to let me just try it, and if anyone complained or if he felt I wasn't getting the job done, we would revisit it. He agreed to my alternative, and it was a win-win for IBM and for me.

The work-at-home arrangement was perfect. I was actually more productive on the days I worked from home. Until then, I never realized how many distractions I had when I was in the office. I think I actually worked harder during this time because I was determined to prove that this arrangement could work, and I didn't want to disappoint Harris by having it fail. On the days I worked from home, I did most of my system work early in the morning before my kids woke up and late at night once they were in bed. I scheduled most of my phone calls during their naptime. It gave me great flexibility in managing my time around my kids' schedules on the days I worked from home while still meeting the needs of the business. I wore a pager so I could always be reached, as this was before cell phones were prevalent. Of course, nowadays, working from home is quite common, but back then Harris and I were a little ahead of our time and early pioneers in venturing into this territory. Harris became a great supporter throughout my career, as well as a mentor and friend. As I advanced in various positions throughout the years, he occasionally reminded me, "And you wanted me to pay you to leave!"

Carol ended up transferring to the West Coast and subsequently left IBM a short time thereafter. My new manager was a black male, Shederick Harrison. This was my first time ever working for a black male. I didn't really know Shed, and the naked truth is that I was a little worried about what he would think of me, as I was somewhat insecure about black men's perception of me since I was married to a white man. I often wondered if they thought I had sold out or that I believed black men weren't good enough for me. These feelings were based on nothing more than my own insecurities. But Shed and I hit it off and worked well together. If he had any personal opinions or views regarding my marital situation, he never let it show or get in the way of our working relationship. It was, as it should have been, a non-issue.

Over the next year, Jim's business grew rapidly. He began expanding the business and opened a second office, in Buckhead, an upscale business district of Atlanta. In July of 1994, while vacationing in France, Jim casually mentioned to me that he was thinking about expanding the business further and opening a West Coast office – in Seattle, Washington. He asked me how I felt about relocating to Seattle for about a year while he got the West Coast operations up and running. I told him I wasn't really sure. Before I left for vacation, Shed, Harris, and I had started having discussions about what position I might take next, as I was approaching the end of my staff assignment. I knew that my next job would be key because it could be the turning point of my career. I felt like I needed to decide if I was really serious about advancing in my *career* or just happy having a *job*. Jim said we could think about him going to Seattle alone while I stayed in Atlanta, but neither of us was thrilled about being physically separated. And he didn't like the idea of leaving me back in Atlanta with two young kids. We tabled the discussion and enjoyed the rest of our vacation.

Like so many things in my life, when events happen, they happen rapidly. By mid-August, Jim made the decision to open the Seattle office. I came home from work one evening, and Jim said, "Honey, I'm moving to Seattle. Are you coming with me or not?" This was not good timing, as

IBM was in the midst of major layoffs, and I knew that getting a transfer would be as remote as winning the lottery. I told Jim that I was definitely going with him, but I might be going without a job. We knew that Seattle was big Microsoft territory, and we had a few contacts there. We decided that I would try to get a transfer with IBM, but I would pursue opportunities with Microsoft at the same time.

I scheduled a career discussion meeting with Harris and dropped the bomb that I was moving to Seattle and wanted to transfer. Harris said, "Lisa – Seattle? There's nothing in Seattle. If you were going to San Francisco, there would be more opportunities. But Seattle just reduced its workforce significantly."

I said, "I know, but since I'm going out to Seattle to find a house, could you please just call your counterpart out there and see if he will have a courtesy interview with me while I'm there?" Harris agreed to make the call, but I could tell that he wasn't too optimistic that I would find an opportunity with IBM in Seattle.

Harris made the call to the Pacific Northwest Trading Area's general manager, Bruce Leader, and Bruce agreed that he would meet with me. But he was very clear that this was simply a courtesy since Harris was emphatic that I was someone whom he should meet, as I had excellent skills. My interview with Bruce was scheduled the same day as an interview I had with Microsoft. My interview with Microsoft went very well, and the company was interested and wanted me to come back for a second interview. I left the interview feeling very confident about my marketability. At IBM, we often devalue our skills and lose sight of how valuable we are outside of IBM.

Prior to my meeting with Bruce, I had done my homework to learn as much as I could about the Seattle office. I knew which major accounts they covered. I understood the demographics of the office and knew that there was a diversity problem from a race and gender perspective. I met with Bruce, and after he shook my hand, he said, "Lisa, it's nice to meet you. I have heard great things about you. But I have to be honest; I'm not sure why we're having this meeting because we just laid off a significant portion of our workforce."

I flashed that huge "make a lion's heart melt" smile and boldly but confidently responded, "But Bruce, you don't really even know me yet. I may have better skills than those people you laid off."

And then, I did something I had never done in my entire career – I played the diversity card. I said, "You have a diversity problem. There are very few women or minorities in this office and Trading Area. Let me take you through my background so you can see where my skills fit and how they can benefit this Trading Area. If you bring me on board, not only do you get a person with great skills, you get another woman and minority to help your diversity problem."

Bruce looked at me almost in awe and said, "Okay, tell me about your background."

As I was going through my career background, I could tell that the wheels were churning in Bruce's head. He listened intently as I spoke with great enthusiasm and passion. I can be quite animated when I am excited. I was full of energy, and I could tell that he was feeling the energy too. After about an hour of back-and-forth dialogue, Bruce said, "Well, you certainly have an interesting background and a diverse set of skills." He went on to tell me that he didn't have any management positions available, but with my Services experience and my technical background, he could bring me on board as a project manager in the Services organization. He said that if I was willing to do that, then once things settled down, we could figure out

124

what to do with me long-term. I told Bruce, "I'll come here and sweep the floors if I have to!" We both laughed and shook hands. We decided that we would make my effective transfer date September 15. That gave me a little less than 30 days to go back and tie up some lose ends in Atlanta.

Jim was very happy to hear that I was still going to be gainfully employed with IBM. I told him about my discussion with Bruce, and Jim was surprised that I had played the diversity card. I had always said that I never wanted to get a job just because I'm a woman or a minority. I wanted to ensure that my gender or race would only be an added benefit to perhaps getting noticed, but I always wanted to feel comfortable that my skills, ability, and track record were what made me competitive.

The next few weeks were pure craziness because Jim traveled often between Atlanta and Seattle getting the office established and hiring people. We had decided that we would keep our home in Atlanta and rent a home in Seattle, since our plan was to return to Atlanta in a year. This Seattle move was supposed to be temporary. If things went well, we planned on my leaving IBM once we returned to Atlanta and casually discussed my working in his business in some capacity. I was busy closing out some things at work and thinking about all the things that needed to get done to prepare for our move.

At this point, we had another live-out nanny, Elizabeth, who was nicknamed Bizzy. She had been with us for about a year. We had known her for quite some time, as she lived around the corner from us and used to baby-sit for us occasionally when she was in high school. She had been out of high school for about a year when she came to work full-time for us. Our kids adored her, and she adored them. They were now four and five and each had developed very different personalities. They were – and still are –

like night and day. I told Bizzy about our plans to move because I wanted to give her as much notice as possible to find another job. She asked me what I was going to do about a nanny in Seattle. I told her that I was working with a Seattle nanny agency to find a new nanny. To my surprise, she said, "If it's okay with you and Jim, I'll move to Seattle with you."

"Really?" I said. "You'd move with us"?

She responded, "Are you kidding? This is my ticket out of here! I love your kids, and I can't imagine them having to get used to a new place to live and a new nanny all at the same time." I told her to discuss it with her parents, as she still lived at home. She assured me that her parents would have no problem with it and that they would be happy for her to have this opportunity.

Bizzy's parents were supportive of her decision to move to Seattle with our family. She was so excited, and I was elated, as finding a new nanny was one less thing I had to worry about. Jim had already gotten Kristin registered for school on one of his trips to Seattle, as she was entering first grade. We decided that we would find a good preschool for Jennifer once we were moved and settled.

Much to my surprise, Jim decided that he would drive across country with the girls alone. Neither of them liked being cooped up in a car for long periods of time, and I knew that there would be the proverbial whines of, "Are we almost there yet?" But he assured me that he wanted to do this. Since he had been gone so much over the preceding couple of years, he thought it would be fun to have bonding time with the girls alone. He planned to stop many places along the way and thought it would actually be educational for the girls. I later found out that on day two of the drive, the girls were quite bored, so he stopped by a Toys R Us. He loaded up the back seat with many new toys, games, puzzles, and books. The girls were as happy as could be. Daddy was a very nice daddy!

As a kid whenever my family would take one of our many road trips, my mom always did most of the driving, as my dad had poor eyesight because of his glaucoma. Before we would pull out of our driveway, my mom would always place a Bible on the dashboard of the car and look up to heaven and say, "God be with us." As an adult, I never did that. However, two weeks after Jim and the girls left, Bizzy and I loaded up my BMW and headed for Seattle. Just as I pulled out of the driveway, I stopped the car, reached into my glove compartment, and pulled out a small Bible I kept there. I placed it on the dashboard of the car, looked up to heaven, and said, "God be with us." Bizzy looked at me sort of puzzled as if to say, "What was that all about?" I shrugged my shoulders and said, "It's just something my mom used to do when I was a kid when we went on long car trips."

Bizzy said, "Well, I have my guardian angel pin on." She showed me a small guardian angel she had pinned to her sweater.

I smiled and said, "Well we've got all the protection we need. We're on our way." We gave each other a high five and I pulled out of the driveway.

It was raining and thundering really hard that day. We were almost to the state line between Georgia and Tennessee when I felt like my mom's psychic abilities had been transferred to me. There was a piece of a tire in the road, and as I went around it, I said to Bizzy, "Well that's going to cause a major accident." No sooner had the words come out of my mouth that my car hydroplaned and I lost control. We were in the far left-hand lane of a four-lane major interstate. My car was spinning out of control 360 degrees across the four lanes of traffic. I looked up and saw a big tractor-trailer heading for a head-on collision with us. I closed my eyes, covered my face, and screamed, "Jesus Christ!" Bizzy was screaming some other unintelligible obscenities. I felt and heard a big bang and then another big bang as my car came to a complete stop. I opened my eyes and saw that we were up against the guardrail of a big downhill embankment. Bizzy very shakily said, "Are we alive?" I answered her in an almost confused manner and said, "I think we are." I looked down at my body and then at Bizzy's expecting to see us mangled and blood-drenched. But neither of us had a scratch. There was no shattered glass and no blood. I asked her if she was okay, and she said she felt fine.

A crowd had gathered around the car, and I could hear people yelling, "Are you okay in there? Unlock the door!" I opened my door and got out of the car. I told the crowd we were fine. A big burly looking man with an extreme Southern drawl said, "Lady, you're one lucky gal. I almost hit you head on with that truck over there." He pointed to the tractor trailer, which was the last thing I remembered seeing before I closed my eyes and covered my face. I said, "But I know I hit someone or something before I hit the guardrail." He said, "Yes, you hit that car up there." He pointed to a Toyota a few feet up the road. There was a woman walking down the road towards us with a flimsy umbrella over her head, and I assumed she was the driver of the Toyota. My assumptions were confirmed as I heard her yelling, "I hope you have good insurance!" The force of the wind and rain inverted her umbrella.

I responded, "I have excellent insurance, but, more importantly, are you okay?"

She said in a very irritated tone, "I'm fine, but I think my car is totaled." I told her I was really sorry, but there was nothing I could have done to prevent the accident. She calmed down a bit and said, "Yeah, it's okay." I then walked around my car to view the damage. The front was absolutely fine, but the back passenger side had a big dent and the rear of the car was completely smashed in. The rear bumper was lying on the ground. For some reason, I instinctively picked it up and threw it in the backseat of the car.

A state trooper arrived and asked me and the other driver, as well as a few witnesses, what happened. Our descriptions were all consistent. He didn't even give me a ticket. It was clear that the car I hit was not drivable and would need to be towed. The officer asked me if I wanted my car towed. I told him that I thought my car was drivable. He said, "Okay, where are you going? I'll follow you for a little while to make sure you feel like the car is driving okay."

I said, "We're on our way to Seattle."

He replied, "You're going to drive this car to Seattle in this condition?"

I responded back, "If the car feels like its driving okay, my plan is to continue on with my trip to Seattle."

He shook his head as if he was amazed or perhaps thought I was crazy, but he said, "Okay. I'll follow you for a few miles."

The car handled just fine and I didn't notice any difference. After following us for a little while, the officer pulled along side my car and I gave him the thumbs up sign indicating that all was well. He gave me the thumbs up back and sped off.

I didn't call Jim until we stopped to eat, hours after the accident. I didn't exactly tell him the magnitude of what happened. I simply said, "We had a little accident, but we we're okay. The car has a few dents, but it's fine." Of course, he pressed me for more details, so I told him, "Well, actually the back end of the car is pretty much smashed in, but the car is driving just fine." He told me that I was out of my mind to drive the car like that across country and that I had no way of knowing if the car was damaged underneath or had a cracked axle or wheel. He told me to just leave the car wherever I was and to get Bizzy and myself to the airport to fly to Seattle. I was extremely stubborn, though. I told him there was no way I was just going to leave my car – we were fine, the car was fine, and I was driving. He was furious with me. I have no idea why I was so insistent on driving. It's just more validation that when I make up my mind to do something – right, wrong, or indifferent – I become pretty determined. In hindsight, driving that car across the country in that condition probably wasn't the smartest thing to do.

Nevertheless, Bizzy and I drove to Seattle without any further incidents. While my car may have looked like we were from an episode of *The Beverly Hillbillies*, it held up just fine. We arrived in Seattle three days later. When Jim saw the condition of my car, he simply shook his head. I flashed my big smile and said, "Honey, at least I kept the bumper." I showed him the bumper, which I had in the backseat of the car and had driven over 3,000 miles across country with.

My car accident was yet another confirmation to me in the power of prayer. I do believe in miracles, as God showed us a true miracle that day. It's as if he had his guardian angels stand between my car and that tractor trailer, as it only missed hitting us head-on by a hair. It would have certainly and tragically ended both our lives. Furthermore, even with all the spinning and banging of my car, that Bible never moved. When my car stopped, I noticed that the Bible was still sitting on the dashboard.

The move to Seattle was supposed to be a new chapter in our lives. I was clearly supporting my husband's business venture and making my career secondary. But it would only take 12 months for us to find that the tables were about to turn.

CHAPTER THIRTEEN

Settling Down and Moving Up

Our family fell in love with Seattle immediately. What a beautiful part of the country it is. Even though we had heard that it rained in Seattle all the time, our first few months there we saw only a small amount of rain. With the backdrop of the Cascades and the Olympia Mountains and the surroundings of Lake Washington and Puget Sound, I found Seattle to be absolutely breathtaking. We immediately bought a boat so we could explore the waters and the islands surrounding Seattle. The girls enjoyed our weekend boat trips, and it was a great way to spend quality time as a family.

After about a month in my job as project manager, I was less than enthused. The services contract I was assigned to manage was boring to me. I liked the people, and I liked the Seattle office, but all the excitement I had been accustomed to feeling in my previous assignments just wasn't there. This was the first job in my IBM career where I woke up each morning and dreaded going to work. I couldn't wait for the weekends to come. After a few months passed with no change in my feelings, Jim and I started having some serious conversations about my resigning. He knew I wasn't happy with my job, and he said he would support whatever decision I made.

Right before the Christmas holidays, I took a couple of days off as vacation. While I was giving thought to what I would write in my resignation letter, I received a phone call at home from Bruce Leader's executive assistant, not to be confused with an administrative assistant. Executive assistants (EAs) at IBM are assigned to senior executives and operate as the executive's right-hand person. EA assignments are typically for high-potential candidates and last for about a year. The EA gains first-hand knowledge about how the business operates and receives experience and exposure that's invaluable. Bruce's EA informed me that she was going to be taking some vacation, and Bruce wanted me to sit in for her. She then went on to tell me that she was moving to a new job in January, and Bruce was interested in having me replace her as his EA. He felt like I had the perfect background. I was stunned. Here I was composing my resignation letter, and it was as if this wonderful opportunity dropped right into my lap.

I did sit in for the EA while she was on vacation, and I got the job as her replacement in January. I loved the job – it reminded me of when I worked in the president's office in college. I enjoyed being on the inside of what was going on. Being still relatively new in the Western Area and virtually unknown, it gave me instant visibility to key executives. Bruce and I worked very well together. Our personalities were vastly different, but they complemented each other. Bruce was low key and very much an intellect, while I was usually bouncing off the walls. Once I got comfortable in the job and with Bruce, I had no problem stating my opinions and views, even if they differed from Bruce's. I earned his trust and respect and felt he valued my opinions, as my thinking was somewhat different from his.

While I was in the job, IBM restructured and did away with its Trading Areas. Bruce became the vice president of Small and Medium Business for the Western Area. It was exciting to me to be able to help structure the new organization. I had a real interest in the small and medium business marketplace because it hit so close to home with Jim being a small-business owner. I began working incredible hours and traveled at times. This was probably the beginning of the turning point in my career, as I was making a conscious decision that I might want to go for it all.

Our kids had adjusted well to Seattle and really liked living there. Kristin was in the first grade and was doing great in school. Jennifer was in a private preschool three days a week. Bizzy was actually able to get a job at the preschool and worked there on the days our youngest attended. This gave her some extra income in addition to what we were paying her. She too fell in love with Seattle. And all was going well with Jim's business.

Toward the end of 1995, a new Western Area general manager came in, Skipp Wyatt. Shortly after he accepted the position, he began making some executive changes to his team. Bruce moved on to a different job, and his replacement was Dan Pelino. I was uncertain as to what was going to happen with me, as it was time for me to move into a different assignment as well. While Skipp had gotten to know me a little as Bruce's EA, Dan didn't know me at all. But the minute I met him, there was that instant connection. I liked him immediately. I could tell that he was a real people person. Our personalities were so similar. I knew I would enjoy working on his team if I had the opportunity.

Jim was ready to go back to Atlanta, as our original plan was to stay in Seattle only for a year. We had been there for a little over a year at this point. But I didn't want to leave. I had no desire to return to Atlanta, for I had truly fallen in love with life in Seattle. I was now pretty serious about my career, and I had a desire to see how far I could go relative to climbing the corporate ladder. While I still had some feelings of working mother's guilt, I rationalized that I would not be a good stay-at-home mom and my kids were better off with me working. In hindsight, I'm not sure this rationalization was in the best interest of my children's needs. It was a somewhat selfish rationalization of my own needs, or perhaps my perception of what I thought my needs were.

Jim was supportive of my decision, and we jointly decided that we would stay in Seattle and follow my career to see where it would take us. He too really enjoyed life in Seattle. Ironically, Seattle has one of the highest populations of interracial couples. We felt extremely comfortable there. Our kids were in an environment where many kids had parents who were from different races or ethnic groups. They did not stick out as being different. Seattle had so much culture. The people there seemed so down to earth, open-minded, and nonjudgmental. I couldn't think of a better place or environment to raise our kids.

In February, IBM held its annual Partner World event in San Diego. This is a major event that our business partners attend to learn about our products and services and to meet with IBM executives. As I was somewhat between jobs, I was asked to attend the event with Skipp Wyatt and assume the role as his temporary EA. I was excited about this opportunity to get to know Skipp better and to attend all of his meetings with our business partners. I was able to get a first-hand view of their issues and concerns and the actions that needed to be taken. Skipp and I talked a lot about the small and medium business marketplace, as that was a key market where we needed our business partners' focus. We strategized on how we could go to market in a more effective and efficient manner with our partners and came up with the idea of doing joint marketing campaigns. Skipp ran this idea by several of our key partners in meetings. They liked the idea. We spent time with Dan Pelino discussing this idea, and he too thought it was the direction in which we needed to go. Skipp and Dan decided that Dan would need a business unit executive with responsibility for new accounts and for the very small business segment of the marketplace. That person would need to work very closely with our partners to develop joint marketing plans for capturing market share. There was no mention of who would assume that role. However, in the subsequent meetings that Skipp and I attended with our partners, he began introducing me as the new business unit executive that would be working closely with them. I was a little stunned by this introduction but went with the flow without questioning Skipp.

Dan and I spent some time together, and he too talked as if this business unit executive role was mine. I finally asked him if I had been promoted to this new job. He told me yes and said that it was obvious to him and Skipp that I had the energy, the creativity, and the right background to be successful in this role. I was ecstatic about the job and about the fact that I would be working for Dan. It was yet another incident in my career of good things just sort of happening for me.

The next several years were some of the most exciting times of my career. I absolutely loved my job and was passionate about what I was doing. Dan had an awesome team of business unit executives (BUEs) that was diverse, with several white males, a black male, a Polynesian, and three women, including me. Dan was a master at motivating his team. He was a great manager and a fantastic leader. He made the job fun and made every member of his team feel valued. He was by far one of the best managers I've ever had in my IBM career.

I was living and breathing IBM. My job did not seem like work to me; it had become a way of life. I had another instant connection with a woman on my team, Diane Jacobs. She and I could almost read each other's minds. She too was so passionate about her work and full of energy and enthusiasm. She and I would often be on the phone late at night crafting out new marketing campaign ideas. We both were night owls and had some of our most creative moments in the wee hours. Sometimes we would be on the phone and I would look at the clock and say, "Di, we're nuts. Its midnight, and here we are trying to solve the problems of the world." She and I became extremely close and remain the best of friends.

The other two female BUEs on Dan's team were awesome. They were Lori Terry, a strikingly beautiful, tall woman with long curly red hair who was responsible for the services portion of the business and really knew her stuff, and Terri Hall, with whom I became very close. In fact, she has become one of my best friends. Terri was extremely smart, and had a very natural beauty about her. While Lori and I were somewhat flashy and flamboyant in our dress and appearance, Terri was like the Ivory Snow girl. She dressed well, wore very little makeup, and wore her hair short to medium in length. She was confident and comfortable with herself. She had responsibility for competitive accounts. All three of us had very outgoing personalities, and we were very good at what we did. I secretly used to refer to us as "Dan's Angels," as we were about as close as you could get to *Charlie's Angels*. In some ways, we were like Dan's secret weapon. Customers and business partners loved us. The three of us could get their attention just by walking in a room. But as soon as we spoke, we captured their full attention because we were smart, credible in our areas of responsibility, confident, and had no problem being heard. We each exceeded our quotas and made great contributions to the business.

By 1998, Dan had moved to a new job in the Storage Systems part of the business. Before he moved to his new job, we began having discussions about what I should do next. There was a lot of discussion about the fact that I should consider going back to the East Coast (New York) so I could get visibility with some of the key corporate senior executives. While I had become well known in the Western Area and had developed a great reputation, I was still an unknown entity to key senior executives back at corporate, where many decisions relative to important positions are made. Jim and I were open to moving, but I still didn't really want to leave Seattle. Terri ended up also taking a job in Storage Systems. Dan was still quite involved in my career, as he had become a significant mentor and advocate for me. There were some marketing opportunities in Storage Systems that were good possibilities for me. I went on several interviews but was less than enthused about the jobs. I actually had a job offer to work for a woman named Margaret Ashida, who in later years became a peer of mine. I turned the job down because I didn't feel like it was the right opportunity for me. Margaret and I have often talked over the years to other young women in the business about that experience and how the fact that my turning the job down because I didn't feel like it was the right job didn't impact my ability to progress in my career. Sometimes saying no is the right thing to do. Many women fear that saying no to an opportunity craters their career, but I feel strongly that saying yes to the wrong opportunity can be detrimental.

I was patient and decided that I would wait for the right opening to surface. My new manager was a woman and was supportive in my efforts to find the right opportunity. Dan continued to stay in touch with me and continued to help me in my search. By May, we found a great opportunity - perfect for my background and for me to develop some new skills. It was a Market Development Executive job in Global ERP (Enterprise Resource Management) Solutions. My marketing skills, my knowledge of the small and medium business marketplace, and my experience in working with Business Partners were critical skills necessary for this job. The job would necessitate a move back to the East Coast, but it would afford me the chance to gain visibility back at corporate, as well as gain international experience because it was a global job.

I interviewed for the job and got it. The general manager assured me that if I did a good job, I would be able to compete for a Director level job within 12 to18 months.

The timing for the move to the New York area was great. The girls were now age eight and ten, and about to get out of school for the summer. The move would allow for some good business opportunities for Jim. While I was sad to leave Seattle, I looked forward to yet another new chapter in my career and our lives. Bizzy did not move with us because she had fallen in love with a young man she met in Seattle. She had practically raised my kids, and we both knew it was time for her to move on with her life. She had become like family to us. In some ways, she felt like an older daughter to me and in other ways like a younger sister.

My new job started immediately, so I traveled back and forth between the East Coast and the West Coast while waiting for the girls to get out for the summer. This was a very hectic and somewhat stressful time. Jim and I didn't want to rush into finding a house, so we decided that he and the girls would go back to Atlanta for the summer as we still had our house there. I would live in temporary housing while trying to find something permanent.

Between traveling to Europe often for my new job and going back and forth between New York and Atlanta, some days I felt completely exhausted. Jim was busy with his business and looking after the girls, so he didn't have a lot of time to help me look for housing. I didn't have much time either, and time was flying by. Jim flew in over the Fourth of July weekend, and we must have looked at 20 houses before finally selecting one. It was an older house on a beautiful four-acre piece of property in Connecticut. I always liked new houses, but Jim assured me that we could renovate the house and make it beautiful. I loved the property and didn't want to keep looking, so I agreed that this house was it. I would later vow to never try to renovate a house again while living in it.

I got the girls registered for school as Kristin was entering the fifth grade and Jennifer was entering the third. We closed on our house in the middle of August, which was perfect as the girls were to start school the end of that month. Kristin was not very happy about this move and the fact that she was leaving her friends and would have to find new ones. The move didn't seem to faze Jennifer. But both girls quickly adjusted to their new environment and new school and found new friends. We hired a new nanny who was from Slovakia. Little did I know that a few years later I would seriously question the huge effect this move to New York may have actually had on Kristin.

I loved my new job and had a great manager, John Herlihy, who was a director. He and I got along great. We worked in a matrix management environment, so while John had many people who took direction from him, I was his only direct report. We operated like a team and more like peers. While I thought I was a high-energy person, John bounced off the walls. Sometimes I would tease him, asking, "John, did you have your Ritalin today"? He and I not only developed a great professional relationship, but we also developed a friendship that we've maintained. John used to tease me and tell me, "Lisa, someday I'll work for you." I used to laugh and dismiss it.

I did well in my job and, after a year, John and our general manager were actively looking for a director level job for me to compete for. Dan was also still very involved in my career and coached me often. Amazingly, just like so many times previously, a wonderful opportunity came knocking at my door, but when it surfaced, I thought I had absolutely no interest. But it turned out to be the opportunity of a lifetime. It was an opportunity to work as the EA to Nick Donofrio, senior vice president of Technology and Manufacturing. I had heard of Nick and knew he was a key senior executive, but I didn't know much about him. When I received the phone call that Nick was interested in interviewing me for the job, my first reaction was "No way." I had already done the EA job, and I had no interest in doing it again. But I was told I should give some serious thought to it, as this was an EA job at a very different level of the business. I immediately called Dan and began venting. I didn't understand why I should accept another EA job. Dan reinforced that this EA job would be different than my previous experience. Nick reported directly to Lou Gerstner, then chairman and CEO during this time. Dan told me that this was a once-in-a-lifetime opportunity that would be extremely beneficial long-term. I trusted Dan, as he had never steered me wrong. I agreed to interview for the job.

Within the first five minutes of meeting Nick during my interview, I was completely sold on the idea that this would be an awesome opportunity. That instant connection was there between him and me. His style and manner impressed me. He was so approachable and came across as very genuine. He told me that he knew I was anxious to find a director level job, but if I took the job as his EA, he would only keep me for about six months. He told me that my job was to be a sponge and observe and learn as much as I could. He offered me the job, and I accepted it. Then I immediately told him that I was about to go on two weeks vacation for a scuba-diving trip and asked if it be okay for me to start after my vacation. He said, "Of course. Go on vacation and have a great time. I'll see you when you get back." I left the interview and was in a state of euphoria.

My EA stint with Nick was by far the best experience of my entire career. I learned more in my time with Nick than I had learned my entire career. The man was simply brilliant. I loved his intellect. Not only was he deeply technical, as he had an engineering background and actually held several IBM patents, but he also was a great people person. He had a management style that was quite different than what I imagined senior executives to have. He was approachable and not at all intimidating. Everyone loved him, he was highly respected, and I never heard anyone say a negative thing about him. He had a passion for helping and supporting women and minorities. He was a real gentleman and very caring. I enjoyed watching him in action, and I was definitely soaking it up like a sponge. After about 30 days in the job, I felt extremely comfortable with Nick. I was beginning to understand his thought processes and how he went about making decisions. I traveled with him and had the opportunity to be in several meetings with him and key customer executives. I felt like I was at the grown-up table. When we traveled together, he was an absolute gentleman – always opening doors for me.

I took on a few projects for Nick that I led and did a good job with, and. I knew that he was pleased with me. I was impressed with his morals, values, and principles. He was a great family man, an awesome executive, and a wonderful person. I even like the way he dressed. I'll never forget the time he and I were on our way to an event where he was going to be speaking. I looked at Nick's attire and started laughing because he and I were dressed almost identically. We both had on olive green blazers, khaki colored slacks, black mock turtlenecks, and brown suede shoes. I felt like I was becoming his clone. Not only was I starting to think like him, I was starting to dress like him too! We both found it funny that we were going to this event looking like twins.

One of things I admired most about Nick was that he not only had great morals and values, but he also acted on those qualities. For instance, one of my most embarrassing moments with Nick occurred when we were attending IBM's annual Partner World event. We had congregated with a small crowd of executives discussing the upcoming IBM Board of Directors meeting. Nick was responsible for determining what would be demonstrated to highlight the state-of-the-art technology we had implemented with some of our customers. We were doing some exciting things with Victoria's Secret at the time, and the discussion centered on whether we would highlight them at the board meeting. In the midst of the discussion, one of the male executives said, "Lisa, do you wear Victoria's Secret?" The crowd went silent, and several of the women actually gasped. My mouth opened but no words came out. Nicked looked as white as a ghost. I could tell he was not too happy by this executive's comment. Nick simply said, "Lisa, let's go." With that, we turned and walked away. I held firm to my philosophy that most people really are good people who mean no harm. I knew the executive who made the comment meant no harm. I really believed that it was somewhat of a Freudian slip. Perhaps he unintentionally said what he had been thinking. Had Nick not been with me, I probably would have come back with something like, "It's none of your damn business." But sometimes saying nothing is best. The comment was no reflection on me; it was a reflection on the executive. I'm sure he felt embarrassed and stupid. I was more embarrassed for him than for me. Later, he sought me out and apologized profusely. I let him know that no harm was done. Ironically, our paths never crossed again.

Nick kept his promise of keeping me in the EA job for only about six months. As I approached my six-month anniversary, I began interviewing for director jobs. Almost six months to the day, I started my new job as director of Distribution Channel Management in IBM's Technology Group. It didn't take long for me to realize that the Technology Group (TG) would be one of the most difficult organizations I had ever worked within. This was the hard-disk-drive and semiconductor portion of IBM's business. The culture in TG was very different, as it was not only white male-dominated, but most of the folks there had engineering or manufacturing backgrounds. But the good news was that Dan and Terri were also part of TG because the Storage Systems business had moved under the TG organization. Dan ran the sales organization, and Terri worked for him. I was initially part of the marketing organization but later reported under sales. I was elated, as I was once again working for Dan.

My most difficult assignment while in TG was developing a new go-to market strategy around the use of e-markets. This was a highly controversial strategy, and not many folks bought into it initially. People felt that it conflicted with our Distributor strategy. Everyday, I felt like I was going to war. But Dan was right there supporting and encouraging me. He would tell me, "Lisa, this is new and different, and people may not understand it. Just take baby steps and spoon-feed it to them." I followed Dan's advice and kept with it, using all of my charm and people skills. Eventually, people started buying into the concept. There were three guys on my team who were responsible for the e-marketplace sales, Jim Walsh, Greg Porpora, and Bob Rohr. These guys worked almost around the clock and had so much conviction and passion about their jobs. They genuinely wanted to see me succeed and were hell-bent on proving the naysayers wrong. They truly believed in what we were trying to do, and while they often got frustrated and felt beat down, I would do fun things to keep them motivated and let them know how much they were appreciated and valued. In the end, we were vindicated, as there was success with the e-marketplace go-to market strategy.

Much of the eventual success of the e-marketplace strategy was due to the support of TG's then CFO, Jim Polus. He fought the hard battles with me and ran interference when necessary. He got to know me well and liked my tenacity and energy. He saw me in action and witnessed me going toe-to-toe with a few executives who fought the strategy. He liked what he saw in me so much that, two years later, in January of 2002, I began working for him as vice president of Sales Operations.

This VP promotion was a tremendous leap of faith in me from Jim Polus and John Kelly, TG's senior vice president. In January 2002, I was actually in Atlanta for my husband's father's funeral. I received a call on my cell phone that Jim Polus wanted to know when I would be back at work because he wanted to set up an interview with me for the VP of Sales Operations position. My initial reaction was, "Why would he want to interview me? I'm not a finance person. I'm a sales and marketing person." In the past, the position had been held by people with a strong finance background. I was told that Jim wanted to do something a little different with the position and was considering putting someone in place with a strong sales and marketing background versus finance. While I was flattered that I was a candidate, I was leery.

When I interviewed with Jim, I spent most of the time trying to tell him why I didn't think I was the right person for the job. Case in point, women seem to often doubt their abilities, but men don't seem to do this. I was really concerned about the fact that I had no finance or operations experience. After much dialog, Jim said, "I'm more convinced than ever that you are absolutely the right person for this job." He made me the job offer, but I told him I needed 24 hours to think about it. By sheer coincidence, I was scheduled to meet with Nick the following day for one of our quarterly mentoring meetings. I told Jim that I wanted to think about it and discuss it with Nick. Jim said, "That's fine. Just come see me right after you talk to Nick."

I met with Nick and voiced all of my concerns about taking the job. He listened intently and then told me he didn't see why this was such a hard decision for me. He told me that if Jim Polus and John Kelly didn't think I could do the job, they wouldn't have offered it to me. I said that I wasn't sure that I wanted to go down an operations career path. He told me that if I took the job and 12 to18 months later decided that operations was not the direction I wanted to go, what was the worst thing that could happen? I would have developed operations skills that would only help me be a stronger marketing or sales leader. His logic made perfect sense to me. I went to see Jim immediately after the meeting with Nick and accepted the job.

The announcement of my promotion into the VP job shocked many people initially. It was the first time in my career I had received a promotion and the announcement of it caught everyone off guard. I couldn't help but wonder if people thought I got the job because I was a woman and a minority. But regardless of race or gender, the shock was understandable, as everyone fully expected someone from the finance ranks to get the job. There was a lot of speculation about who would be the new VP, and my name was not even a blip on the radar screen. However, Jim did an excellent job making the announcement and made it clear that he selected me for the job because of my strong sales and marketing background. He was not the least bit apologetic about it. He felt that we needed to make some sales operational changes and thought that my leadership and background would ensure it happened. Once people understood the rationale for having a sales and marketing person in the job versus a finance person, it made sense to them as to why I had gotten the promotion.

I had become well respected in TG and had developed a solid track record. But there's no doubt about it, I was very scared about this new job. In addition, my predecessor and I had completely different management styles and completely different personalities. He was highly skilled in finance and operations and had a reputation of being ruthless. But I had a lot of respect for him even though I didn't always agree with his approach to things. I knew that if I put my ego aside, I could actually learn a lot from him. In my first 30 days in the job, I did call him on several occasions to pick his brain. I didn't always take his advice, but some decisions I made were often as a result of his advice.

I had an awesome team of five directors who reported to me, and another who took direction from me. I made it clear in my first interaction with them that I had no intention of trying to fill my predecessor's shoes. I told them that I knew they were all highly skilled in their areas of expertise, and I didn't need to tell them how to do their jobs. However, what I brought to the table was a different perspective, and if they learned to trust me, we would be able to facilitate some changes that would allow them to do their jobs even better. I knew they were all a little skeptical of me at first, but I used the same approach and management style that I had always used. While I challenged their thinking at times, I made sure that they each knew how much they were valued and appreciated. I learned as much from them as they learned from me. Within two months of being in the job, I started to get the same positive feedback that I had grown accustomed to hearing throughout my career, "Lisa, you're one of the best managers I've ever had."

Within six months of being in the job, IBM made the decision to sell off our hard-disk-drive business to Hitachi where half of my organization was now going. This was a very stressful time for me, as TG had gone through multiple layoffs. I would lose sleep at night worrying about the folks who were going to be told that they were being laid off. I took it personally and had a hard time detaching myself emotionally. There's absolutely nothing pleasant about telling someone that they no longer have a job. It didn't take long for me to see the handwriting on the wall that after the sale to Hitachi and some restructuring of the remaining organization, there wouldn't be a need for my position. No one had actually told me that I may be out of a job, but it looked fairly obvious to me. I proactively engaged in discussions with Jim Polus and John Kelly, informing them that I thought I should start looking for a new job. While I had enjoyed my stint in sales operations and learned a lot, I really did want to get back into a sales or marketing position. While John Kelly was emphatic that I would not be out of a job and he did not want me to leave TG, he was supportive of my decision to start looking for a sales or marketing position outside of TG.

I engaged my network of supporters, and together we started looking for opportunities. I ultimately took a job as vice president of Channel and

Alliance Solutions Marketing in IBM's Systems Group. It was a great opportunity for me, but the timing could not have been worse. I didn't realize it then, but I was already into "the perfect storm" of life. I was battling a blood disorder that I had ignored and had no idea how physically ill I was. My personal life was turning upside-down. My emotional well-being was at serious risk. I was running on empty in all dimensions of my life. My mind, body, and soul were completely shutting down. But I kept trying to keep going and was running on pure adrenaline until, one day, I simply couldn't even get out of bed. I knew I had to make some serious changes in my life, and I knew I could not meet the demands of an executive job with everything else that was going on. I went on a medical leave of absence and felt extremely guilty about it. I felt like I was letting everyone down. So many people had gone to bat for me, and I couldn't help but feel like I was disappointing them all. But the guilt didn't matter at that point. I was at such a low in my life that I knew I was going to either die from my illnesses or take my own life.

It would take a long time to rebound, and it was a long and hard battle. But that fighting spirit surfaced once again in me, and I thank God that I'm still alive to tell the story. Intermingled in the midst of my career were so many warning signs that life was not as perfect as it seemed. As I reflect back now I can't help but think, *how could I have been so blind?* The weather alerts had been flashing for a long time that a storm was brewing. But it would take being in the eye of the storm before I even knew what hit me. It almost drowned me and swept me away, but I grabbed hold of a lifeline and started pulling myself in before it was too late.

CHAPTER FOURTEEN

Early Warning Signs of an Impending Storm

There's no doubt in my mind that the hardest job I've ever had is that of being a parent. There is no formal training for this job, and while I have read numerous books over the years on this subject, my performance as a parent was definitely by trial and error. It has been by far the most important and most significant job of my life. And yet, as someone who went through school and college as a straight A student, I would have to grade myself as a D+ at best at being a parent. I thought I was doing A work, but now as I reflect back over the years, I realize I was simply fooling myself. I broke the cardinal rule of parenting – consistency. There was nothing consistent in our household other than Jim and me arguing about what the rules were relative to our children and how to discipline them.

Our children learned at a very young age that "no" did not mean "no" in our home. "No" meant maybe. They learned that if they badgered me long enough, I would give in, and "no" would become "yes." It was a fatal parenting error, and one that I have paid for dearly. Jim and I always seemed to be on opposite ends of the spectrum. I thought he was too harsh on the girls, and he thought I was too easy. I would use the excuse that they were just children and thought he expected too much from them. I, on the other hand, tried to overcompensate for my working mother's guilt and would buy them everything, unconsciously trying to substitute material things for my lack of time shared with them. Most of our arguments were about the kids, and our children quickly learned how to pit Mommy and Daddy against each other. It was a vicious cycle and a dangerous one.

While Kristin was the "perfect" baby, she turned into what seemed like a little monster after the birth of Jennifer 18 months later. I would often describe her to other people as being extremely high-maintenance. It seemed that nothing I did for her or with her was enough. She was very demanding, and I quickly dismissed it as her being a spoiled brat. Actually, I now understand that she was simply trying to get my attention for a long time, and even negative attention was better than no attention at all. By the time she was two, I often worried that something was wrong with her emotionally. The naked truth is that there were times when I really wondered if she was possessed by the devil, something I'm not even sure I really believe in. But I could always make up excuses and rationalize that her somewhat extreme behaviors were just a phase. After all, no parent wants to believe that there is something wrong with their child.

As I reflect back over the years, I now have to seriously question several incidents that may have had a much bigger effect on my daughter than I thought at the time. Any of these incidents alone can be rationalized as no big deal. But the sum and culmination of these incidents is what now haunts me, as I believe they caused actual trauma that manifested itself in other ways over the years.

When Kristin was a little over two years old, we experienced something together that scared me practically to death, so I can only wonder what the effects were on her. Jim had already left for his office, and I was getting dressed for work and waiting for our nanny to arrive. Jennifer was still asleep in her crib, and Kristin was in my bedroom playing while I was in the bathroom applying my makeup. Unbeknownst to me, my daughter was playing with the telephone and inadvertently dialed 911. The dispatcher could quickly tell that it was a child who could barely talk. I learned later that the dispatcher was asking her to go get her mommy. But Kristin repeatedly said, "Mommy can't." The dispatcher assumed something was wrong and that this child was calling for help.

Police were dispatched to our home. Apparently, when Jim had left for his office, he left the garage door open. While the door from our garage to our house was unlocked, the front door was locked. Two squad cars pulled into our driveway, but I didn't hear them. They came to the front door and rang the doorbell, but again I didn't hear it. They then let themselves into the house through the unlocked door from the garage. Again, I heard absolutely nothing, a scary thought within itself. As I stood in the bathroom only clad in my bra and underwear and applying mascara, I heard a loud male voice yell, "Freeze! Police!" I practically poked my eye out with freight as I became frozen. My heart was pounding so hard I thought it was going to jump out of my chest. I slowly turned my head and saw two police officers standing in my bedroom doorway with guns drawn and pointed at me. I actually raised my arms above my head, fearful of getting shot, and said, "I live here. What's going on?"

I think the officers quickly surmised what had happened, as Kristin was sitting on my bedroom floor near the phone, with the receiver lying on the floor next to her. They placed their guns back in their holsters, and I grabbed a towel to wrap myself in. One of the officers said, "Sorry, ma'am. A child called 911, and we thought there was a problem here. We rang the doorbell, but no one answered." I ran over to Kristin; she was still sitting on the floor almost looking shell-shocked. I picked her up, and she began crying hysterically. I know her little mind could not comprehend what had happened. I can't fathom what she must have thought seeing two police officers standing in that bedroom with their guns pointed at her mommy.

As I tried to comfort her, saying, "Everything's okay. Mommy's here," while I stroked her back, the towel wrapped around me fell down, and the police officers quickly turned away as if they were embarrassed. I walked into my closet still holding my daughter, grabbed my bathrobe, and put it on. I walked downstairs with the officers while still trying to reassure my daughter. There were two other officers at the bottom of the stairway. The officers asked me a few questions and then apologized for scaring me but told me they were following normal procedure when there's a question of someone's life being in danger. I apologized to them for the mix-up and saw them out.

Kristin would not let me put her down. Her little heart was pounding so hard I could feel it thumping next to mine like a ferocious drum beat. Our nanny arrived very shortly after the police officers left. I told her what happened and tried to put Kristin in her arms so I could finish getting dressed for work. But my daughter threw an absolute tantrum, screaming and kicking hysterically, saying, "Mommy! I want Mommy!" I took Kristin from the nanny and could tell that this child was petrified, perhaps traumatized. I told our nanny that I would stay home from work and she could have the day off. It took about two hours for my daughter to finally settle down. For the rest of the day, she clung to me like static. She would not let me out of her sight. I don't know if that experience has anything to do with why Kristin has an extreme dislike for the police to this day. I can only wonder if there were long-term psychological effects caused by that frightful experience. After all, police officers are supposed to be the good guys, the ones who protect us. But her first encounter with the police was seeing them point a gun at her almost naked mommy while yelling, "Freeze!"

By the time Kristin was three, she already struck me as being extremely independent, always wanting to try something by herself without anyone helping her. She often used the phrase, "I can do it by myself." But ironically, even with her insistence of doing something by herself, she would lose interest really fast and give up if she couldn't master a task on her first attempt. If she wanted me play a game with her or do a puzzle, she would quickly change her mind once we got started and would want to play or do something different. This was often frustrating to me because it seemed like nothing held her attention without her quickly becoming bored. Whenever I was feeding or holding Jennifer, Kristin seemed to resort to her worst behavior. It was as if she would do anything she could to cause me to have put the baby down and turn my attention to her. But I never realized how observant she really was until we had another scary incident that actually threatened her life.

I used to keep medication in the cabinet above the sink. This was a high cabinet that even I had to use a chair or stool to reach. We had child safety latches on all of our cabinets, including this one. My daughter had seen me repeatedly stand on a stool and push the safety latch to the side to open the cabinet. She had watched me push the supposedly child-safe bottle cap down on various medications. It never dawned on me that at the age of three, she too could figure out how to open the cabinet or get the top off of medication. I underestimated her abilities considerably.

I returned home from work, and the nanny had already fed both kids. Jim was still at his office, and it had become routine that he would not arrive home until late, as his business consumed almost all of his time. After seeing the nanny out, I did my normal routine of taking both kids upstairs to my bedroom to allow them to play while I changed clothes. Jennifer was quite content in her playpen exploring several toys. After a few minutes, I thought it odd that Kristin was awfully quiet. I was in my closet and couldn't see her, but I would normally hear her chattering away. I called her name, and she didn't respond. I came out of the closet and noticed that she was no longer in the bedroom. I went across the hall to her room and then to Jennifer's room, but she wasn't there either. I ran downstairs into the kitchen and gasped when I saw her. She had used a chair to climb on the counter and had opened the safety-latched cabinet. She was sitting on the counter with an empty bottle of children's Benadryl next to her. I have no idea how she managed to actually open the Benadryl. Her shirt was covered in it, and it was dripping down her mouth and chin. I opened her mouth and could tell by her breath and her red tongue that she had swallowed the medicine. But I had no idea how much she had swallowed and how much had actually spilled. She said very proudly, "Mommy, I took my medicine all by myself." I scolded her and was racking my brain trying to remember how much Benadryl had been in that bottle.

I was almost panic-stricken but tried to remain calm. I picked her up, grabbed the phone, and called our pediatrician but got the answering service. When I told the answering service what happened, they instructed me to call

Poison Control because they would instruct me on whether or not to induce vomiting. Poison Control told me not to induce vomiting; they instructed me to take her to the emergency room immediately and to not let her fall asleep. I distinctly remember the words, "Whatever you do, do not let her fall asleep because she may not wake up." I dashed upstairs and grabbed Jennifer out of the playpen while still holding Kristin. I quickly got Jennifer in her car seat but decided to put Kristin the front seat with the seatbelt around her. I was afraid that having her in the backseat in her car seat might cause her to fall asleep. I wanted to be able to keep one hand on her to shake her to keep her awake. On the way to the emergency room, I did everything I could to keep her awake. I tried to get her to sing with me, I made funny faces to make her laugh, but it was obvious that she was getting extremely drowsy.

When we arrived at the hospital, I didn't even park the car. I simply pulled in front of the emergency room, left the car running, and grabbed one kid in each arm and ran in the hospital yelling, "My little girl swallowed an entire bottle of Benadryl!" A nurse took Kristin out of my arms, put her on a stretcher, and began checking her vitals. A security guard informed me that he was going to move my car for me. I followed the nurse as she rolled my daughter into one of the small rooms. A pediatrician and another nurse quickly came in and began asking me what seemed like a million questions; "How much Benadryl did she swallow? Was the bottle full? How did she get to the Benadryl? Where were you when this happened?"

My responses were in rapid succession; "I don't know. I don't know. She climbed up on the counter and opened the cabinet. I was in my bedroom, and she was there too, but she wandered downstairs." The other nurse was rattling off my daughter's vitals, but I couldn't tell if her vitals were good or not. She kept gently nudging my daughter saying, "Stay awake, sweetie." The doctor was giving orders to the other nurse, but I didn't understand any of the medical terms. They began hooking Kristin up to a machine and explained to me that it would monitor her blood pressure constantly. I was concerned that she was not crying and did not seem the least bit upset by this whole ordeal, which made me realize that she had become severely drugged and was out of it. The doctor explained to me that they were going to induce vomiting by giving her a cup of Ipecac to drink. I realized that I was questioning his medical expertise when I said, "But Poison Control told me not to induce vomiting." He very politely said, "That's because she has to be closely monitored to insure she doesn't aspirate once vomiting begins." They got her to drink the thick syrupy drink, and they handed me a big metal bowl to hold under her chin as one of the nurses took my baby out of my arms. I asked, "What's going to happen next?"

The doctor said, "In just a few minutes she will start vomiting violently. Be prepared, it will be like a scene from *The Exorcist*."

I couldn't really appreciate his sense of humor at that moment, but I understood the imagery. Within about a minute and with no warning at all, Kristin began to projectile vomit which seemed to last an eternity. I thought I was going to start vomiting too. She was gagging and coughing, and then she started screaming and crying. I kept telling her, "Its okay. You're going to be okay."

At the end of the ordeal, the doctor informed me that he needed to ask me a few more questions so he could complete some paperwork, which is normal procedure when an accidental drug overdose of a child occurs. I answered all of his questions, taking him through the details of how we ended up in the emergency room. I once again felt like the worst mother in the world, just as I had felt when Jennifer almost died from pneumonia. I didn't know then that I would have those same feelings multiple times over the course of my children's lives. I was supposedly such a smart and competent person, yet when it came to motherhood, I felt totally incompetent at times.

By the time Kristin was five years old and in kindergarten, she was quite a handful. She had already developed this propensity to want to be with kids at least two to three years older than her. She was considered by her kindergarten teacher to be extremely bright. She could already read fluently and could phonetically sound out just about any word. She even could navigate her way around on an old computer we gave her. She had absolutely no behavioral problems at school, nor did she demonstrate any attention-span deficiencies. She was cooperative and one of the smartest kids in her class. But at home, she developed an attitude like the world revolved around her. She often would throw temper tantrums when she couldn't have her way. Although we had taught her to say "please" and "thank you," she often acted downright rude, snatching things out of my hand versus waiting for it to be handed to her.

On her first day of kindergarten, I wanted to drive her to school, but she insisted that she was a big girl and wanted to ride the school bus, which stopped right in front of our house. She didn't even want Jim or me to stand at the bus stop with her, as she wanted to stand there with the other kids whose parents all watched from their doorsteps. Jim and I stood on our front porch and watched our little princess get on the bus. She looked so pretty with her little flowered dress on and her long curly hair glistening in the morning sun. She waved goodbye, and I immediately got in my car to follow the bus. I don't know if I was being overprotective or not, but I wanted to make sure that she arrived at school and got to her class okay.

She had already gone to orientation and knew which classroom she was supposed to go to. But that didn't matter to me; I wanted to have peace of mind by actually seeing her get to her class. When the bus finally arrived at the school, I parked my car and tried to stay hidden from her, following at a distance. There were many teachers standing in front of the school directing the kids to their classes. When Kristin got to her class, her teacher was standing in the doorway waiting to greet her. The teacher saw and recognized me and said to her, "There's your mom. Say goodbye to her." Kristin turned around and looked at me as if she had seen a ghost. She had that defiant look of *what are you doing here; I can do this by myself.* I blew her a kiss, and she gave me a weak smile and waved goodbye, but I remember that look of disappointment on her face. I left her school feeling a little heartbroken.

I can't help but wonder now if that incident gave Kristin an early observation that I was overbearing, overprotective, or perhaps that I didn't trust her. Or, in a weird way, maybe she started to believe that it was okay to tell a lie if you are protecting someone. After all, I had assured her that she could ride the bus and go to school alone on that day. But she looked up and there I was. She must have felt so betrayed.

When we lived in Atlanta, there was a 10-year-old girl who lived down the street from us, and Kristin became quite fond of her. The little girl occasionally came over to our house in the evenings and acted somewhat like a mother's helper. She would play with Kristin and was great at entertaining her. But what started out as an occasional visit became an everyday occurrence. I didn't think too much of it, but Jim became concerned that Kristin's favorite playmate was someone five years older than her. I monitored the interaction between her and the little girl and never saw anything inappropriate during their interactions. In my mind, the little girl was acting somewhat like a big sister. She was always very polite, and I thought that she was a good role model for Kristin.

One Saturday, the little girl came over to play and then asked me if Kristin could go to the skating rink with her and some of her friends. I initially said no, but then the begging and pleading began from Kristin. The little girl assured me that she would watch her carefully and that it would be a lot of fun. I called the little girl's mother to find out if she was going to stay at the rink with the kids. She told me that she would be there and she would be sure to keep an eye on Kristin. She told me that her daughter adored my daughter and felt a great sense of pride in acting like a big sister to her.

They say that mothers have great instincts, and I should have followed mine because I really didn't feel comfortable about my decision to let Kristin go skating. But as usual, I gave in against my better judgment. When she returned home, I could tell that something was wrong. I asked her if she had fun. She said yes – it was a lot fun. But she had that look on her face like something was really bothering her. She told me that she was tired and wanted to go to bed. I helped her with her bath and got her tucked into bed, and we read a story together. She was unusually quiet, so I asked her, "Honey, did something happen at the skating rink that upset you?"

She started crying and said, "Yes, but I can't tell you. I promised I wouldn't tell."

"Sweetheart, you can tell me anything. What happened?"

"They told me something bad would happen to me if I told you."

"It's okay, honey, you can tell me. I won't let anything happen to you," I said. Kristin began sobbing and told me that some of the kids went outside at the skating rink to smoke cigarettes and they let her try it. She said she didn't like it, and she almost choked. They laughed at her. She asked me if she was going to get cancer and die. I assured her that she was not going to get cancer and die. I told her what they did was very wrong, and I was so sorry that it happened. She asked me if I was mad at her. I told her that I was very mad at her friend. I then asked, "Is that all that happened? Did anyone touch you inappropriately?"

"No," she said, "but I just want to go to sleep. I'm tired." I kissed her goodnight and rubbed her back for a while until she fell asleep.

I was furious with myself for trusting her friend and her friend's mother. I called the little girl's house and was told by the little girl that her mom was not home. I questioned her about what happened and told her that I was very disappointed with her. She started crying and told me that she was very sorry, that it wasn't her idea. It was her friends' idea. I told her to never come to our house again. I hung up the phone and felt mortified that Kristin had already been subjected to smoking peer pressure at the age of five.

In later years I often wondered if something more than what Kristin told me happened that day at the skating rink. Over the years, she occasionally mentioned to relatives that she had a big secret, but she never divulged what the secret was. In later years, even through years of therapy, her secret has remained buried deep inside of her, although she has alluded to being sexually molested with no detailed memories of whom, when, or where. My intuition tells me something more catastrophic happened that day at the rink other than her smoking a cigarette. But I have no way of really knowing. I'm haunted by the possibilities and continue to beat myself up for allowing her to go in the first place.

When we moved to Seattle, both of our kids were young enough – four and six – to not have the move affect them. Kristin loved her school, and we lived in a neighborhood with many kids her age. But again, instead of wanting to play with the kids her age, she wanted to play with the older kids. Jim and I became increasingly concerned over some of her behaviors. She seemed to speak without giving any thought to what she was saying. She would often say the most inappropriate and often embarrassing things in front of company. She had a wild and vivid imagination and loved to make up stories that she would later confuse with reality. She often put us on the spot by asking if someone could spend the night even after just meeting them. She had this consistent pattern of acting out at home but behaving like an angel at school.

Even though people would tell me that I was lucky that my girls were so close in age because they could play together, I didn't feel lucky at all. Our girls never really seemed to get along very well. Their personalities and interests have always been vastly different. While Kristin has always been outgoing and the social butterfly, Jennifer has always been introverted and fairly shy. Our girls would fight often, and it bothered me that they appeared to have a general dislike for each other. Kristin constantly wanted to be entertained and could drain the energy out of an Energizer battery. But Jennifer has always been content to entertain herself and preferred to be alone. She developed exceptional artistic abilities at a very young age and could spend hours drawing, painting, or coloring. However, I noticed that Kristin had great difficulty assembling even the simplest toys. When we would go to McDonalds, we always ordered the Happy Meal for the kids. Jennifer could assemble the toy with no problem and would always assemble the toy for Kristin, as she would get frustrated and say, "I can't do it." While I didn't think too much of this at the time, it was yet another red flag that something was wrong.

During first through third grades, Kristin did exceptionally well in school and was predominantly an A student. Her teachers always described her as extremely bright and always commented that she seemed much older than her age. Her second grade teacher once commented, "If I didn't know better, I would swear your daughter had been in this world before." His comment was very interesting to me, as several family members had made that same comment about her over the years. Up to this point, my mom had mentioned to me on several occasions that she believed Kristin displayed symptoms of hyperactivity and attention deficit disorder. But I dismissed it because her behavior problems seemed to occur only at home, not at school. I now know that I was in denial. Looking back, all the red flags were there that this child was at serious risk emotionally based on her frequent outbursts, her unusual behavior patterns, and her difficulty in processing instructions or putting things together in a logical order.

By the fourth grade, it became more obvious that there was a problem. Kristin's grades declined significantly, and she seemed to lose interest in school. And her behavior at school began to change: she became disruptive in class, often speaking without raising her hand and engaging in constant talking that distracted the other students. Her teachers were quite concerned over this sudden change in her academic progress, as well as her school behavior. She would often tell her teachers, "Our family is different. My parents don't care what I do. Besides, they're never home anyway. They both work all the time and travel all the time." She had already developed the perception that our work was more important to us than she was. While Jim and I did travel frequently, we rarely were both out of town at the same time. But in hindsight, perhaps we depended too much on our nanny to take care of our kids and didn't understand then the long-term implications it had on Kristin. While we showered our kids with genuine love and did many things as a family on weekends, it wasn't enough for her.

I must admit that during our Seattle years, I was very much into my career. As I mentioned previously, I lived and breathed IBM. I was definitely guilty of showering our kids with material things that I thought would make them happy. I was simply trying to overcompensate for my low self-esteem relative to motherhood. I felt very inadequate as a mother, often feeling pulled in too many directions. By the time I came home from work I would be drained and often just wanted to be alone. The buying of material things backfired with Kristin, though, because she developed a lack of appreciation for anything. She didn't take care of her things, and if she lost something or broke it, she wasn't fazed because she knew that mommy would go buy a new one. Again, it became a vicious cycle that had significant consequences in later years.

Toward the end of Kristin's fourth grade year, her teachers began to suspect that she had a learning disability. We were asked for permission to test her, which we concurred with. She however, scored quite high on the aptitude test they gave her. In fact, they were surprised by the results because in most subjects, her aptitude was in the range of seventh through ninth grade. The school year was ending, and it was decided that they would do more testing at the beginning of her fifth grade year. However, we moved to the East Coast that summer, and the testing was never completed. What I didn't know then that I understand completely now is that aptitude and learning disabilities are mutually exclusive. A child can have a high aptitude and still have a severe learning disability. In fact, it's a major red flag when a child scores high in aptitude yet performs poorly in school.

Our move to the East Coast affected Kristin in multiple ways. First of all, by 10 years old, girls become very cliquish. Their identity is often tied to who their friends are and how well they're accepted by those friends. She was very sad to leave her friends in Seattle and was frightened by the thought of going to a new school, starting all over in making friends as the new kid. Also, while our kids' school in Seattle was quite diverse, we moved to a small town in Connecticut that had virtually no racial diversity in the town or in the schools. It was lily-white. For the first time in either of our daughters' lives, they suddenly felt out of place. Kristin was constantly asked by other kids if she was black or white. She endured some of the same teasing that I remembered as a young child, being called names such as "half-breed" and other derogatory racial slurs. Jennifer was in third grade, and at that age, perhaps kids are more tolerant of differences, as she seemed not to experience these problems. But I had always been very candid with our children, telling them that people can be very cruel, and being of mixed race, they might encounter unintelligent people in life who may not accept them. But I used the same principles with my kids that my parents always instilled in me, that they could do anything they wanted to do in life. I constantly reinforced that "One shouldn't be judged by the color of their skin but by the content of their character."

Our first year living in Connecticut was very hectic and stressful, as I traveled out of the country often for business. We were in the midst of renovating our home, and Jim was doing many of the renovations himself while still trying to run his business. I often felt angry because living in a chaotic, torn-apart house is not the easiest thing to do. It seemed as if I had too many balls in the air and my life was a constant juggling act. Even with hired help, someone still has to manage the help, and that usually falls on the woman's shoulders, no matter how helpful a husband might be. Kristin did not like our new nanny very much and did everything she could to make her life miserable. At work, I was the shining star who appeared to have everything together. But at home, I was turning into an absolute witch and often took my frustrations out on my kids, my husband, and the nanny. I felt tired all the time, and I felt resentful too. Nothing Jim did was good enough for me, and I turned into the constant complainer. Jennifer was doing great in school, but Kristin was struggling. I became increasingly frustrated because her teachers' comments began to sound like a broken record over the next few years – *Your daughter is very bright and intelligent, but she's lazy and puts in no effort.* I would later come to regret that I listened to her teachers' comments for the next two years like it was music to my ears instead of challenging them. I wanted to believe that there was nothing wrong with Kristin. Jim and I in turn put even more pressure on her and rode her hard regarding her relatively low performance in school. We enrolled her in the Sylvan Learning Center for tutoring three days a week, and while it helped some, she continued to struggle academically. Her grades continued to drop.

By our second year in Connecticut, Jim had scaled his business back considerably and actually took a job as an executive in a software company. This was a major turning point in our lives, as now he commuted to New York City and traveled frequently, being very wrapped up in his career. I was consumed in mine, as I was now the EA to Nick Donofrio, and our lives had become a tangled web of travel schedules, the kids' activity schedules, more home renovations, and social and business engagements. And in the midst of it all, our frustrated nanny abruptly quit. Looking back, I can't say that I blame her for quitting. I didn't realize it then, but she was living with a very dysfunctional family. Jim and I argued constantly. The girls argued and fought with each other; they also were rude to the nanny. I was often mean to the nanny, and I often criticized how she did things. I had become jealous of her relationship with Jim, as they got along well and he would often defend her against my criticism. In his eyes, nobody could do anything right by my standards. Nothing anyone did was good enough for me. I had become miserable, and I was making everyone else in our house miserable too. It seemed like Jim and I had engaged in a competition of whose career was more important. We had both become selfish. Meanwhile, Kristin was about to enter into a dangerous stage in her life, and neither Jim nor I saw it coming.

At work, everyone admired me, and I constantly was asked by other women what my secret was to doing it all and having it all – the career, the husband, the kids. I looked ten years younger than my actual age, I always managed to look almost flawless, and I always had that effervescent smile on my face. Little did they know that all was not as perfect as it seemed. My "secret" was that at home I felt like a complete failure at motherhood, and I think my husband felt like he was living with the Wicked Witch of the East. Work had become an escape for me. The worse things got at home, the more time I wanted to spend at work. Sad, but it's the naked truth.

As I reflect back, it's so obvious to me now that Jim and I fell into the common traps of dual-income professional couples. We were both going for the gusto, trying to reach the pinnacle of "success." The more we achieved, the hungrier we got and the more we wanted. The more money we made, the more we wanted to make. I ask myself now, *how much is enough?* I thought that money and material things made me happy, but the happiness was only temporary. I continued to feel miserable, angry, resentful, and confused. I can't speak for Jim, but I now know that I lost sight of the important things in life. My priorities had gotten way off base, and I was breaking all of my own principles regarding keeping harmony between life and work. My kids had become almost incidental to me. I rationalized that they were well cared for, had the best of everything, were well traveled, and were lucky to have this great life that so many other kids only dreamt of. But I was so wrong. The clouds were forming, and the storm was just around the corner. My life was about to be flooded with rain, and I had no idea then that if I didn't jump into a life raft, I was going to drown.

CHAPTER FIFTEEN

The Formation of the Storm

I went into my first director level job at IBM in 2000 with things chaotic in my personal life, but I thought that I was coping well. Kristin was now in middle school and had barely gotten through sixth grade with passing grades. She was becoming increasingly frustrated with school and was withdrawing from us. In August, prior to seventh grade, we were at the pediatrician for her routine physical. I almost fell out of the chair when, out of the blue, she said to the pediatrician, "I think there's something wrong with me. I've done some research on the Internet, and I think I have obsessive compulsive disorder (OCD)."

The pediatrician asked, "Why do you think you have OCD?"

Kristin responded almost in adult like fashion, "Well, ever since I was little, I've always had compulsive thoughts. I have a lot of rituals, like counting my socks over and over again and touching certain things in a precise order before I go to bed. I can't concentrate, and I feel confused all the time. School is really hard for me. Everyone thinks I'm smart and just lazy and I don't try. But I do try really hard, but no matter how hard I try, I just don't understand my schoolwork. I know there's something really wrong with me."

The pediatrician asked me to step out of the room so she could speak to Kristin alone. When she had me come back into the room after having Kristin step out, she informed me that she thought Kristin did have some serious emotional issues that needed to be dealt with. She said the symptoms my daughter described did sound like OCD. She recommended a child psychiatrist and told me to make an appointment for Kristin immediately.

Prior to this incident at the doctor's office, we went through a series of nanny nightmares. After our Slovakian nanny abruptly quit, I quickly found a new nanny through a newspaper ad. This new nanny was from Soviet Georgia and had only been in this country for a short while and spoke very little English. I interviewed her, liked her, felt that special connection with her, and hired her. I'm embarrassed to admit that I've spent more time researching the features of a new car than I spent researching the background of this nanny. But I was in a state of complete desperation. My mom has always said, "God looks out for babies and fools." God was definitely looking out for this fool, as I hired this complete stranger to come live in our home, care for our kids, and pretty much manage the day-to-day operations of our household while knowing very little about her. But she turned out to be wonderful, and both of our daughters liked her a lot. She was very sweet and very conscientious about her duties, even if she did roll Jim's truck on her second day of work!

We had a fairly new Volkswagen Beetle, which was for the nanny's use. The Beetle had a manual shift, and I didn't want the new nanny to drive it until I was sure she knew how to shift gears. Jim had a Dodge Ram pickup truck, which we used for towing our boat. On our nanny's second day of work, she wanted to go that evening to visit another nanny who was a friend of hers. I told her that she could drive the truck and I would check her out in the Beetle the next day. She had been gone for about an hour when I received a phone call from a state trooper informing me that our nanny was fine but had an accident and flipped the truck over. I could not believe what I was hearing. She apparently turned a corner too fast; the road was icy, and she lost control of the truck and it flipped over. No one else was involved in the accident and she escaped without a scratch, but she was very shaken up. The state trooper drove her home, and she was visibly shaken. I gave her a hug and told her the most important thing was that she was okay. She was crying and said in very broken English, "You no fire me?" I assured her that I was not going to fire her and that accidents happen. But I told her she had to be extremely careful driving in the future – my kids' lives would be in her hands.

There were no more car incidents with the new nanny, and things were working out very well with her and us. But I'll never forget the night Jennifer's pet parakeet, Sunshine, which she had had for a couple of years, suddenly died, making her extremely upset. I comforted her for a while and told her to try to get some sleep because it was extremely late. But it was the nanny who heard Jennifer still crying in her bedroom later that night. She went in and laid in bed with her, holding her and telling her that it was all going to be okay. As I stood at Jennifer's bedroom door observing this scene of the nanny comforting my daughter and showing her genuine love and concern, I felt very conflicted. While it touched my heart, it broke it at the same time, as I was thinking, w*hy am I not in there lying with my daughter instead of the nanny?* It was yet another incident that left me feeling quite inept as a mother. I'm not making excuses, or maybe I am, but it was if I couldn't detach my work persona from my personal life. At work, I had learned to keep my emotions in check, acting somewhat cold or indifferent at times with the tough skin often necessary to survive as an executive. I couldn't seem to turn that persona off in my home life.

As I continued to juggle the demands of work and life, I attended weekly therapy sessions with Kristin and the child psychiatrist who was treating her. He had diagnosed her just as she had diagnosed herself, having OCD. Week after week, I sat in the psychiatrist's office in horror listening to my daughter detail her feelings, many of which had to do with her perception of me and our relationship. I learned so much about her and myself, and what I heard scared the life out of me.

Just as I was engaged in what seemed like the middle of a war with the e-market strategy I was leading at work, the new nanny informed me that she was in love and was going to leave us to go live with her boyfriend in New York City. She had been with us for four months at this point. However, the good news, she informed me, was that she had a good friend in Soviet Georgia who was about to come to this country and would be looking for a full-time nanny job. If it was okay with me, she would have her friend take over the job. She said she would stay on for two more weeks to help with the transition and to give us an opportunity to see if we liked her. I said that it was fine, and I couldn't help but think with sarcasm, *Jim will be thrilled to learn that he's now going to be living with five women for a short while in our house.* He had already mentioned on several occasions

171

that it seemed like our girls, the nanny, and I were PMSing all at the same time. I figured, what was one more to add to the gang for a few weeks?

The new nanny arrived on the scene, and we all immediately liked her. Our current nanny showed her the routine, and her friend had no problem learning the ropes. She also spoke English well. As it turned out, she was a phenomenal classical pianist and could make our piano practically sing. On the weekends, she would often play the piano before Jim and I were out of bed. We would lie in bed listening to her play, feeling as if we had our own private concert hall and were being serenaded by a gifted classical pianist. I would sometimes look at her sheet music, and even though I can read music quite well, her music was so complicated it gave me a headache just trying to read the notes.

Even though we all liked the new nanny a lot, by her third month with us, we all felt that she was a bit of a prima donna. I started to feel as if I worked for her, as she was somewhat demanding. Not to mention that she was practically eating us out of house and home. Our grocery bill suddenly doubled. One of her responsibilities every week was to do the grocery shopping while the girls were in school. Even though I would make a shopping list, week after week I would find that our refrigerator and pantry were stocked full with the foods she liked, which nobody else in the house liked or ate. We had a hot tub on our patio that she rather enjoyed, and we had no problem with her using it. However, it seemed like whenever Jim and I would go out to relax in the hot tub together, she would be in it and would stay there, giving us no privacy, as if it didn't dawn on her that three's a crowd. She asked if she could take on a few piano students to make some extra money, and I told her it was fine as long as her teaching schedule didn't conflict with our schedule. But week after week, there seemed to be multiple conflicts. When I casually voiced some concern about it, she was indignant and told me that I needed to have a more predictable schedule. And then, the straw that broke the camel's back was the constant disagreements regarding her international phone calls and the fact that she felt she shouldn't have to pay for them. She was racking up phone bills in excess of $100 a month and felt like that should be a perk of the job. After her fourth month with us, I finally told her that she needed to find another job. Her demands were outweighing the benefits we were receiving, and I had come to feel like I was a guest in my own home.

I'm not completely crazy, though, for I already had a backup plan. Our previous Slovakian nanny had remained in touch with me, and she and I had made our peace with each other. I had actually met her for dinner a few times, and she confided that she was quite unhappy with the family she had gone to nanny for after she left us. She informed me that while she thought we were a little difficult to live with, she realized that we had actually been extremely good to her. She said we treated her more like family, but this new family treated her strictly as hired help. I can proudly say that we have always treated our nannies as part of the family, often taking them on vacations with us and inviting them to participate in family outings and social events. She was miserable and was begging to come back but was honest and said she that was planning on going back home to Slovakia in six months. I told her that I was about to get rid of our current nanny, and she could come back as long as we could reach some compromises on some of our previous disagreements. We discussed the compromises, and I gladly took her back. She entered our lives, and this second go-around was great.

As Kristin's seventh-grade year progressed, she struggled both academically and emotionally. I had several formal meetings with the principal and her team of teachers, voicing my concerns about her academic struggles. I asked several times that she be tested to see if she qualified for special education. I had already informed them at the beginning of the school year that she had been diagnosed as having OCD and was under the care of a child psychiatrist. I even signed a release giving her guidance counselor permission to speak to the psychiatrist so that her teachers would understand how best to work with Kristin. I later learned that they never bothered to speak to the psychiatrist. I explained to the teachers, as the psychiatrist had explained to me, that Kristin's symptoms of OCD were mental versus physical. Often, children with OCD will do things like wash their hands constantly or erase on their paper excessively, leaving a hole in the paper. Kristin did not exhibit these characteristics. Her obsessions were mental. If the teacher said something she didn't understand, she would become obsessed with that one thing and would not hear anything else the teacher said. If she was taking a test and came across a question she didn't know the answer to, instead of skipping it and moving on, she would become obsessed with that one question and would not complete the rest of the test. The principal and the team of teachers reinforced that they did not believe testing was necessary and did not think that my daughter required special education. They again stated that she was very bright and intelligent but was lazy and just didn't put in the required effort to do better. I became increasingly frustrated, as I was getting nowhere with the school. I would later learn that not only did the school violate my daughter's civil rights by refusing to test her, but they also had not followed some of their own processes and policies regarding dealing with a child with suspected learning disabilities or emotional problems.

Our Slovakian nanny went back home to her country after staying with us for six months. Jim and I had already decided that we would have no more live-in nannies. Our girls were now old enough to where we didn't need childcare as much as we a needed part-time housekeeper to manage the household and drive the kids to their various activities. In all honesty, I felt like I needed a part-time wife. I found one, too, and she was great. She was a little older and more mature than our previous nannies. She kept the house clean, did the laundry, went grocery shopping, dropped off and picked up the dry cleaning, ran various errands, and drove the kids wherever they needed to go. She was an excellent cook, providing near gourmet meals at least three times a week. On the rare occasions when Jim and I had to be out of town on business trips at the same time, she would stay overnight. She was almost too good to be true, and after being with us for almost a year, we found out she *was* too good to be true. She suddenly stopped showing up for work and disappeared with our Volkswagen Beetle!

In the month before she disappeared, she had a lot of problems with her own car. She knew that I was trying to sell the Beetle, which we no longer needed. She asked if she could buy it. I agreed to sell it to her for a lot less than what it was actually worth and agreed to deduct a small amount of money out of her weekly pay as car payments, but I let her go ahead and take the car. I drafted a contract detailing our arrangement, and we both signed it. After a month of this arrangement, she simply failed to show up one day and became unreachable, even though I had provided her with a cell phone that I paid the monthly charges for. When she failed to show up the following day and was still unreachable, I actually started frantically calling every hospital in the area thinking that perhaps something had happened to her. I finally called a friend of hers whose number I had. Her friend informed me that she had just seen her that day and she was fine; she had no idea why she wasn't showing up for work and was avoiding my calls and messages. Finally, after two weeks of not hearing from her, Jim and I showed up at her house with the local police and repossessed the car. Her only explanation was, "I'm sorry, but people like you don't understand people like me." I had no earthly idea what she meant or what she was talking about. She called me a few days later and told me that she had the rest of the money for the car. I told her to bring me a certified bank check and I would gladly sign the car over to her. She showed up with the check and told me she had lost the cell phone. I signed the car title over to her and told her to have a nice life. We've never seen or heard from her again. She would be the last nanny we would ever have.

My life was steadily becoming more and more complicated. Now, with no domestic hired help, I felt as if I never had time to breathe and was exhausted all the time. Jim and I were constantly juggling our schedules to ensure that one of us could get the girls to wherever they needed to go. Things around the house were piling up, and even though everyone was taking on more household responsibility, the bulk of it fell on my shoulders. The girls were now coming home from school for the first time ever with no adult supervision. While at their ages, 12 and 13, this was not that uncommon for other children, it was a major change for them. I started leaving the office at more reasonable hours, but then I would log on to my computer late at night after the girls were in bed and sometimes work until 1:00 or 2:00 in the morning. I would get up at 6:00 AM and start the routine all over again. I became more and more sleep deprived, and I became crankier as the days passed. I didn't know it at the time, but I had a serious blood disorder that could have been fatal if left unchecked. Jim was often out of town on business trips, and sometimes I felt like a single parent. I was lethargic and had no energy, but I kept going nevertheless.

Kristin and I continued with her weekly therapy sessions, and I became increasingly aware of what she thought of me. While I thought I was being a good role model for my girls by having a career and showing them that a woman can achieve just as much as a man can, this was not her perception at all. Tears ran down my cheek as I listened to her tell the psychiatrist, "The most important thing in my mom's life is her job. If my mom didn't have her work, I think she would actually roll over and die." She then proceeded to say, "I don't think my mom likes being a mother. I think she tries to spend as much time as she can at work to avoid being with us." My heart was simply shattered. And then, as if to deepen the wound, my daughter went on to say, "My mom and dad are overachievers, and they're very successful in their jobs. Both I think they are terrible parents. My little sister is very smart and everything comes easy to her. No matter what I do, I'll never live up to my parents' expectations. I'll never be as smart as my sister. I'm the black sheep of my family, and nobody seems to care how I feel."

Jim had actually gone to a few therapy sessions with Kristin, and quite frankly, he had a hard time taking seriously some of her comments. He said he sat there feeling like he was in the middle of a *Seinfeld* episode. My personal opinion is that Jim, like me, was in denial for a long time that our daughter had some serious issues. I was starting to come to terms with it, but he had not. After all, this was his firstborn, his little princess. But instead of Cinderella, she was turning into Courtney Love.

In the midst of all this drama in my life, my father had several strokes, each leaving him more and more incapacitated. His health was steadily declining, and I was flying back and forth to Miami to see him. I couldn't stand to see my father in the condition he was in. He had always been such a strong man, and to see him lose so much weight, unable to see, walk, or barely talk, was more than I could handle. He no longer had control of his bladder or bowels and had to wear adult diapers. I had always been a daddy's girl and felt like my dad would always be there to protect me and help me anytime I needed him to. But there I was, bathing him, changing his diaper, and feeding him as if he was an infant. It was a heart-wrenching experience. I would always leave Miami and cry the entire flight back home, wondering if the next time I saw my father, *would he be in a casket?*

Toward the end of Kristin's seventh-grade year, she became great friends with a boy in her class who also seemed to have some issues of his own. They talked on the phone constantly, and if he wasn't at our house, she was at his. They did everything together, and both of them seemed to lose interest in the sports they had previously participated in and in other friends. Jim did not approve of this relationship, as he didn't feel that this boy was a good influence on Kristin. But for the first time in a long time, she seemed happy to me. Jim and I had many arguments regarding her spending time with this boy. It became a vicious triangle – Kristin would come to me and get one answer, and her father would give another. Jim started getting increasingly frustrated with our home situation. He felt like he was becoming a nonentity in our home and that I was making all the decisions relative to the girls with little regard for what he thought. It was the beginning of what almost became a destroyed marriage.

By the summer of 2001, I became completely frazzled. My marriage was unraveling rapidly, and Kristin now seemed to be in a world of her own. She appeared to be shutting us completely out of her life. She began lying frequently, and when I would try to talk to her, she would tell me to stay out of her life. She started spending more and more time locked in her bedroom, and she now had a group of friends that neither Jim nor I approved of. She would argue with us that nobody was ever good enough for us. She became increasingly disrespectful and downright defiant. The handwriting was on the wall that she was about to spiral out of control.

I was under considerable pressure at work, as TG was undergoing the first of what would become several layoffs. I had people I was about to lay off, a daughter who seemed to despise me and whom I didn't seem to even know anymore, a marriage that was falling apart, a father who appeared to be dying, and a younger daughter I was trying to keep sheltered and protected from all the chaos in our house. I rapidly lost weight on my already small frame and couldn't sleep or eat. I was a walking zombie. The clouds were definitely forming, and "the perfect storm" was just around the corner. Just when I thought things couldn't get any worse, the storm surged.

CHAPTER SIXTEEN
The Perfect Storm

I've always believed that God puts people in our lives for a reason. I'm more convinced of this than ever because in 2001, as I was in the midst of "the perfect storm" of life, the assistant I had, Mary Ann Barry, was a true godsend. Not only was she an exceptional assistant with a keen eye for detail, but also at times she was like my mother, my sister, my friend, my spiritual advisor, and my confidant. As my professional life and my personal life had become one big tangled web of scheduling, Mary Ann not only managed my day-to-day work schedule, but she also helped me manage my life. I had come to completely trust her, and she knew every intimate detail of my life. I could not have managed without her knowing, as my work meetings and appointments would often have to be readjusted to accommodate therapy sessions with Kristin, my own doctor appointments, meetings with the school, and sometimes spur-of-the-moment flights to Miami, as I would dash there when I thought my dad had taken a turn for the worse. Mary Ann knew me perhaps more intimately than anyone at IBM, and she was the first to recognize that I was losing it. I knew she was genuinely concerned about me.

It was two weeks into eight grade for Kristin's. I was just about to walk into an important meeting with Jim Polus (TG's CFO) and several people from a California-based company who had flown in to work with us on our e-market strategy. Mary Ann ran down the hall to get me. As I was about to walk in the door to the conference room, she informed me that Kristin's principal was on the phone and said that it was urgent that she spoke to me immediately. I went to my office, closed the door, and picked up the phone. My heart felt like it stopped beating as the principal said, "Mrs. Whaley, this is Mrs. Hartman. Your daughter is fine, but she's been involved in a serious disciplinary incident at school and you need to come to the school immediately."

I responded, "What kind of incident? What happened to my daughter?"

She repeated, "Your daughter is fine, and I can't tell you anything more other than it's imperative for you to come to the school now."

I told her I would leave immediately, but it would take me about 30 minutes to get there. I hung up the phone, and my mind was spinning with all sorts of thoughts. I could not fathom what on earth had happened, particularly since she said that my daughter was fine.

I told Mary Ann I had to leave, and I dashed into the conference room to tell the people who were waiting for me that I was so sorry but I had a family emergency and had to leave. I asked one of the guys who worked for me, Jim Walsh, to take over and run the meeting for me. Everyone looked at me with great concern and said they hoped that everything was okay and to "go ahead and get out of here." I literally ran out of the building to my car. What should have been a 30-minute drive from my office to the school took me only 15 minutes. I must have been on autopilot, as I got to the school and didn't even remember driving. I couldn't remember if I had stopped for traffic lights, stop signs, or what. My mind was totally consumed with every possible scenario of what could have possibly happened with my daughter.

I went into the administrative office and was told to have a seat and that Mrs. Hartman would be with me shortly. I sat there for what seemed like an eternity, and the waiting infuriated me. I told the assistant, "I want to see my daughter now and want to know what's going on. I left an important meeting, as I was told to get here immediately. I'm tired of waiting." The assistant was actually quite kind and assured me that it would only be another minute. Mrs. Hartman came out to greet me and took me into a conference room, but my daughter was not there. She then went on to tell me something that I had never imagined in all the various scenarios I had conjured up in my mind. My daughter had been caught with marijuana in her backpack and had been accused of actually trying to sell it. Apparently, while riding the bus to school, my daughter had informed some other students that she had some pot in her backpack. Once they arrived at school, a couple of girls went to the office and informed the counselor. My daughter's locker and backpack were subsequently searched, and a small bag of marijuana was found, along with five dollars. In her locker were a series of notes between her and the boy who had become her best friend. The notes looked very incriminating, for they contained a list of people who were interested in buying, times and places they could meet, and a log of potential earnings. At first glance, these notes made it look like my daughter and the boy were serious drugs pushers at the age of 13.

I sat there in utter disbelief listening to the principal talk. Even with all the challenges we had undergone with Kristin, I had not a clue or even a suspicion that she was using drugs. She and I would talk openly about sex and drugs, and she would admit to me that she knew people who used drugs but assured me that she had never tried it. She had even completed the mandatory DARE program at school during sixth grade and had actually won a medal for having the best essay on why kids shouldn't do drugs. The principal went on to tell me that Kristin had been questioned repeatedly and had several versions of where she got the pot, ranging from finding the bag in the school parking lot to a high school boy having given it to her. She told me that the other boy (my daughter's best friend) was found with a marijuana pipe in his pocket and his father was in the next room. My daughter and the boy were each in separate rooms with guidance counselors. She then went on to inform me that the police were there and in just a few minutes the police officer and my daughter would joins us so that he could question her in front of me.

I could feel my blood pressure rise, and my heart was pounding. I was experiencing every possible emotion, from complete anger and disbelief to great sadness at this turn of events. Kristin walked into the room accompanied by a police officer, and she took one look at me and started crying. I said to her, "I can't believe this. What on earth were you thinking? What happened?" Between her sobs, she said, "Mom, I'm so sorry, but I found it in the parking lot and I didn't know what it was." I knew she was lying. As I had absolutely no experience with criminal law, I then proceeded to interrogate my daughter with the principal and the police officer, actually assisting them in getting my daughter to incriminate herself. I had no attorney present, and I had no idea then that this was not just a school matter; this was a serious legal matter. The police officer used all the questioning tactics that I had seen on TV shows such as *Law and Order*. He went back and forth between our room and the room that my daughter's friend was in with his father, telling each that the other one had already told the truth about what happened. After several rounds of this tactic, their stories finally matched.

As I sat in a cold hard chair in that room, there were moments when I wanted to reach across the conference table and wring my daughter's neck. Then there were moments when I wanted to take her in my arms and tell her that it was all okay and we would work through this. But I did neither, as I was numb with not knowing what to believe, what to think, or where we would go from here. The principal then rattled off the school's zero tolerance policy and informed me that Kristin was being suspended for 10 days and would be referred to the Board of Education for mandatory expulsion. She told me that there would be a Board hearing that Kristin and I would need to attend, and I would receive a letter with the details of the time and date. Then the police officer informed me that he was issuing a summons, and Kristin would need to appear in juvenile court. I think that's when the severity of this situation hit me. Again, having no experience in these matters, I didn't know if my daughter would ultimately be arrested and sent to juvenile hall. I now was thinking that I needed an attorney for my daughter.

The principal and the officer briefly left the room, and I called Jim on my cell phone to inform him of what had happened. He, like I, was in disbelief. He was not happy about the situation and the fact that she had been caught with marijuana. But the fact that she had been accused of trying to *sell* it is what totally infuriated him. Why on earth would she do that? Was it really true? Were these incriminating notes just another example of her vivid and wild imagination, as she would often write about things that she fantasized about but never acted on? Kristin and I left the school. When we arrived home, we went into the kitchen where Jim was sitting. It was not a pretty scene. There was a lot of yelling, screaming, crying, and name calling, which quite frankly I'm not proud of. Jim and I were both out of control overtaken with rage. Looking back, I wish I could take back some of the things we said to Kristin that day.

She went to her room, and Jim and I sat for a while talking – arguing. It was the beginning of what would become the blame game that we would each play over the next year. It was my fault because he didn't approve of this boy who probably got her into all of this in the first place, and I had let her continue to see him. I would say it was his fault because maybe if he wasn't so hard on her, then she would have higher self-esteem and wouldn't feel as if nothing she did was good enough. We went around and around blaming each other, screaming at each other, and it was obvious that we were both saying extremely hurtful things that neither of us really meant. It was unproductive, and it wasn't going to solve anything. We were like two wounded bears with a wounded cub trying to figure out how to survive and protect her without getting eaten alive by prey.

I went back to work. I had left so hurriedly that all my belongings were still there. On my drive to the office, I tried to shift my mind back into work mode, but I had a million thoughts going through my head. I wondered how the meeting went that I had so abruptly left. Did we get all of our issues resolved? I thought about what I would say to people, as I knew they would want to know if everything was okay with my family emergency. I thought about the fact that I had to find a good juvenile attorney. How do you ask anyone if they can recommend one without divulging why one is needed in the first place? I thought about Jennifer and how we would explain this all of to her and what kind of effect it would it have on her. I thought about Kristin and tried to imagine what she was feeling. I knew that she was scared to death. I thought about my marriage and wondered if this was the beginning of the end. And then I thought about my mother and could almost hear her voice say, "Lisa, just pray about it. God will see you through this." And that's exactly what I did for the rest of the car ride back to my office. I prayed, I wept, and I starting singing "Amazing Grace" at the top of my lungs.

I arrived back at my office and told Mary Ann what had happened. She told me that she had gone through many things with her boys when they were teenagers and to keep my faith. I would get through this. We talked about the power of prayer and the fact that God never gives us more than we can bear. It was toward the end of the workday by this time, and I stayed at the office only long enough to find out that the meeting I had missed had gone well. I packed up my belongings and left to go back home.

Jennifer had already heard an assortment of rumors regarding her sister on the bus ride home from school. Rumors ranged from her sister had been arrested for drug possession and was in jail to she was a drug addict and pusher and was going to be sent to jail. Jim and I explained to Jennifer what had happened. She was very angry and upset with her sister. She cried and said, "She ruined our family's reputation." I told her that everybody makes mistakes sometimes and the important thing was that we have to hold our heads high, get her sister the help she needed, and not let this destroy us.

That night, Kristin and I had a long talk. She was very distraught and said she was so sorry. She admitted that she had just begun to experiment with marijuana and had only smoked it a couple of times with her friend. She said, "Mom, everybody does it." She swore to me that she had never sold it or attempted to sell it. She said the notes between her and her friend were just them trying to act like they were cool and it was all make believe. She said, "Mom, the $5.00 in my backpack was not from selling drugs. You gave me that money for lunch. Don't you remember?" She was correct; I did give her $5.00 that morning for lunch money. She then went on to say that she knew she had made a big mistake, but everybody was overreacting as if she had murdered someone. I told her that she couldn't minimize what had happened, and it was much more serious than she may have thought. I told her that when we met with the attorney, it was vital that she tell the attorney everything, and it had to be the truth. I told her the attorney wouldn't be able to help if she didn't tell the truth. She promised me she would tell the truth. I hugged her and told her I loved her very much and kissed her goodnight. As I turned to walk out of her room, she said, "Mom, I'm really sorry I disappointed you and Dad."

I worked from home the following day and, in between a full load of conference calls, I started calling what seemed like every juvenile attorney in our area. I had a hard time finding a juvenile attorney that could represent Kristin - the first five I called already had full caseloads. I didn't realize that such attorneys were in such great demand. I finally called a large firm and found one who said she would take the case. We discussed the fee and set up an appointment for Kristin and me.

The fact that Jim could not make himself available the day we were to meet with the attorney proved to be a recurring theme throughout the next few months as we dealt with this fiasco. It became quite clear to me that this was somehow my problem. He was extremely busy with work and acted as if I wasn't. But it was more validation to me that even though I had a career that was just as important as his and made an income as much as his if not higher at times, when it came to resolving unpleasant issues concerning the kids, it fell on my shoulders. As much as women want to believe that we can have a marriage that is 50/50, after talking to many women, I'm more convinced that it rarely works out that way in reality – whether we want to admit it or not.

Kristin and I met with the attorney, and after detailed questioning, she explained what we could expect - that the Board of Education would in all likelihood expel Kristin. Past history with this Board had shown that they were quite serious about the zero tolerance policy. The length of expulsion is what would be in question. She went on to explain regarding the legal matter that Kristin would most likely be placed on probation since this was her first time ever being in trouble. The possession charges would most likely be dropped since the amount of marijuana she was caught with was not enough to be charged with possession. While I don't recall the amount she was caught with, in all honestly it was more like marijuana residue. The major question was whether she would be charged with selling. There was not evidence of her actually selling marijuana, as after many kids were questioned at the school, no one admitted to her trying to sell them marijuana. The most incriminating evidence against her comprised the notes between her and her friend. And even the notes could be questioned as to whether they contained actual events or just fantasy. The attorney went on to explain that the supervisor of juvenile probation would set up a time to meet with Kristin, Jim, and me. Following that meeting, a court date would be set.

About a week later, Kristin, our attorney, and I attended the Board of Education hearing. Prior to the hearing, we had met with the principal, assistant principal, and the Board's attorney. We had all reached an agreement that an appropriate punishment would be for my daughter to be suspended for the remainder of the semester. However, once we were in the Board hearing, I was flabbergasted when the board rejected that recommendation, as they felt the punishment was not harsh enough. They expelled her for a full year. I could not believe that this 13-year-old child was being kicked out of school for a full year. The last thing she needed was to be was out of school with even more free time on her hands. Yes, she did commit a serious violation, and, yes, she needed to be punished. But this was a child who had never been in trouble and had a clean discipline record other than three minor infringements – drawing on her desk, wandering the halls without a hall pass, and refusing to take a test with a substitute teacher. If anything, I felt a more severe and effective punishment would have been to make her go to school an hour early and stay two hours later every day for the rest of the year.

Not only did the Board expel her for a full year, but she also was not allowed on the school campus under any circumstances. This meant that she would not be able to participate in athletics - basketball and soccer in her case. Even though Parks and Recreation sponsored these sports, they used school premises. She was also required to undergo drug counseling at our expense, as well as submit to monthly random drug testing. Because she was under the age of 16, the Board was required by law to provide some form of education for her. Her education would be provided with homebound tutoring two hours a day, and an adult, such as me or my husband, would have to be home when the tutoring occurred. I felt as if we had all just been given a death sentence.

After the Board hearing, my head was spinning with thoughts of what life would be like for the next nine months. How would we manage this tutoring arrangement with both Jim and I working? How would we juggle our schedules to ensure one of us was home? What was Kristin going to do all day long with no school, no socialization, and no sports activities? She was going to be like a prisoner in her own home.

The following week, Kristin, Jim, and I met with the supervisor of juvenile probation. We went through an intensive interview, and Jim actually became irritated, as he felt like we were on trial and weren't the ones who had committed a crime. The supervisor interviewed Kristin alone and then came to the conclusion that she was not a professional drug dealer as the school had made her out to be. It was his conclusion that this was an immature child who had gotten caught up with the wrong set of friends and was trying to live out some fantasy without giving thought to what she was really getting herself into.

The next few weeks were pure craziness, as I was still trying to meet the demands of my job, trying to find a drug-counseling program for Kristin, and trying to get the tutoring arrangement scheduled. And Kristin's court appearance was coming up. My marriage was steadily unraveling, as I had become angry at Jim and somewhat resentful that he was not helping me with any of these arrangements. It was all on me. We were barely talking to each other, and most communication resulted in arguing. And to make matters worse, my father's health was steadily declining.

I asked the principal if the money that the Board was spending for homebound tutoring could be applied to a special or private school for Kristin. I was concerned that this child was already struggling academically, and I still questioned whether or not she was learning disabled. I felt adamant that two hours a day of homebound tutoring would not be effective for her and was inadequate. The principal informed me that she would relay that request to the superintendent. A week later, I received a formal letter from the superintendent informing me that my request was denied. As far as I was concerned, it was a "slam, bam, thank you ma'am" with no suggestion that we meet to discuss why I felt the homebound tutoring would be inadequate and no suggestion that we conduct a formal

Planning Placement Team (PPT) meeting. I would later learn that, at the very least, a PPT should have been conducted since my daughter's school records contained numerous red flags that she was at risk emotionally and academically – something the Board had blatantly ignored during our hearing.

I began frantically trying to find a private school for my daughter to attend at my own expense, but to no avail. Most were already full, as this was now a month into the school year. Three schools that weren't full would not accept her. After all, what private school wants to accept a child with less than a stellar academic record who had just been expelled for possessing drugs? Parents send their kids to private schools to get away from kids like my daughter, don't they? In reality, that's a joke because private schools have just as much of a drug problem as public schools. In fact, kids in private schools often have more access to money and more access to drugs. No school is totally drug free. It's just the sad reality of the society we live in today.

Consequently, we proceeded with the homebound tutoring, and, at the tutor's suggestion, we agreed to have it conducted at the public library. We thought that this was a good idea so Kristin could have some semblance of a routine everyday. But it still meant that Jim or I would have to transport her. Kristin's court appearance took place, and the possession charges were dropped, but she was charged with conspiracy to sell. She was placed on nine months' probation. Her probation would entail a visit every other week by a probation officer and random drug testing. During the probation officer's visits, Jim or I would need to be home.

Over the next eight months, my schedule was a total nightmare, and I started to feel extremely stressed out and pulled in too many directions.

Kristin was in weekly therapy sessions with a drug counseling psychologist for adolescents. During each of her sessions, she spent time alone with the psychologist, I spent time alone with him, and then my daughter and I would spend time together with him. Between the demands of my job; the schedule shuffle of Kristin's therapy sessions, tutoring sessions, and probation officer home visits; and Jennifer's activities (I was still trying to keep her as sheltered as possible from all of this), I felt like I was working 24 hours a day. Anything work-related that didn't require face-to-face or phone interactions, such as e-mail, I would do at night. Jim rearranged his schedule and traveled a little less and worked from home more. I was living the ultimate façade, giving the appearance at work that everything in life was great and coming home to a dysfunctional household. The truth is that I had come to dread going home. I would stay at the office as late as possible to avoid facing the truth.

Kristin's tutoring was an absolute disaster. The first tutor seemed not to have a clue as to what she was supposed to be doing. There was much confusion about what curriculum she would follow, how tests would be handled, and who would issue my daughter's grades. After a few weeks, the tutor informed me that my daughter was very difficult to work with, as she seemed unmotivated and depressed. I was informed a few days later by the school that there was going to be a tutoring change. The second tutor was a man, and he was actually quite good with Kristin. However, even he stated that she was very far behind and it was as if the first tutor had done nothing with her. He engaged in playing catch up with her. But seeing how this was almost three months into the school year and Kristin had come to feel like a total outcast with no friends and virtually no social life of a normal 13-year-old, she pretty much gave up and just didn't care about anything anymore.

She hated her therapy sessions and would often comment that she was tired of talking about and dwelling on the same things over and over again.

I could tell that she was becoming increasingly frustrated and depressed. Even her probation officer was concerned that she was becoming somewhat disengaged in life. The probation officer felt that having her out of school was the worst thing for her. But the juvenile criminal court had no say in the Board of Education's decision. The psychologist was also concerned that Kristin just didn't care about anything anymore. He too felt that having her in almost total isolation would do more harm than good. She had no friends, and even though we put her in guitar lessons and tried to do things with her to keep her busy, she was bored out of her mind. What 13-year-old wants to do everything with her parents?

Nevertheless, we muddled through the next few months and got through the holidays, giving the appearance that everything was just fine. I was embarrassed about our situation and only told family and a few very close friends what was going on. We decided to spend Christmas in Atlanta with Jim's family and actually drove there. The drive to Atlanta was in fact fun and the best time we had had as a family in a long time. We had one of our best Christmases ever and all took great pride in helping Jim's father learn how to use the Internet with the new computer he had gotten for Christmas. Even though my marriage had been strained, Jim and I put our differences aside, and it seemed as if there was still a small spark left in our relationship. When we left Atlanta to drive back to Connecticut, we had no idea that it would be the last time we would see Jim's father alive. He died suddenly of a massive heart attack in late January. We were all shocked and devastated.

January was bittersweet for me. I was excited about my new promotion to vice president of Sales Operations, but in hindsight, it probably wasn't the best time for me to take on such a significant challenge. Jim's father's death had a major effect on him, and he was completely grief-stricken. My father had yet another stroke, and this one left him almost totally incapacitated. He developed pneumonia, and the doctors did not expect him to pull through. I once again dashed down to Miami, expecting that I too was about to lose a father.

Over the next couple of months, Kristin sunk deeper into a depression. She was miserable about her situation, and she was making everyone else in our house miserable too. Tutor number two abruptly couldn't tutor her anymore, and we were now starting on our third. This third tutor, however, Diane Welsh, was a godsend. Not only did she connect well with Kristin, but she also seemed to genuinely care about her. She did her best to work with Kristin and get her caught up. This was a woman strong in faith, and as she got to know me over the next few months, she would talk to me about the power of prayer. She encouraged me to go back to the church that I had once attended. There was a new minister there now, and she thought I would like him a lot. She became somewhat of a mentor for Kristin, and Kristin came to really trust her.

Jennifer was doing well in school, but she became an innocent victim of her sister's sins. She was tired of other kids, and teachers for that matter, asking her questions about her sister. She started to hate going to school and begged to go to a different school for the next term. I promised her that she could attend private school. She couldn't wait for the summer to come. She was excited about the private school that she had applied and been accepted to.

By the summer, Kristin had found new friends, but these were friends who had also been in trouble and not a crowd that we approved of. But her choice of friends was limited. After all, the "good kids'" parents did not want their kids to associate with her. We lived in a small town, and the word had spread that she was into drugs. She was "damaged goods" as far as other parents were concerned.

Toward the end of the summer, Kristin's probation ended and she had passed all of her random drug tests. I petitioned the superintendent to allow her to start school at the beginning of her ninth grade year versus waiting until the second week of school, which would have been her start date based on the full year of her expulsion. The superintendent agreed. I was ecstatic and thought that just maybe we would get back to some normalcy in our lives. Little did I know that the worst was yet to come.

I had just gone through the stresses of laying people off from work and the sale of our hard-disk-drive-business to Hitachi. I felt tired and weak all the time. Mary Ann would comment to me that I didn't look like myself. I felt sick all the time but thought it was just stress. I had no idea when I took yet another new job as Vice President of Channels and Alliance Marketing that I was seriously ill with a blood disorder.

In September the new school year began, and Jennifer was euphoric about starting at her new private school where she would not be in her sister's shadow. Kristin was both excited and frightened about starting high school and getting back into a normal school routine. While Jim and I were still together in terms of living under the same roof, we were more like two ships passing in the night. While we were fairly polite to each other, we were not together at all. He had pretty much disengaged from the girls and me and was basically a nonentity in our house.

Two weeks into the school year, I received a call from the superintendent. She informed me that she had just gotten the results from a drug test Kristin had taken back in July, and it tested positive for marijuana.

She said that this violated the conditions for her early admission back into school and she would need to remain home for the next two weeks. I became enraged and asked her what we were going to accomplish by taking her out of school for two weeks when I was doing my best to get her reengaged. Since every preceding drug test had been negative, as well as the test for August, it was possible that the July results were in error. But she didn't want to listen to anything I had to say. I told her, "It's obvious you're doing everything possible to keep my daughter out of school instead of trying to help her." We exchanged some unpleasant remarks, and I informed her that she would hear from my attorney. Strictly on impulse, I hung up on her. I lost all respect for this superintendent as an educator, as an administrator of the school, and as a person.

When I informed Kristin that she was once again out of school for the next two weeks, it was the beginning of an absolutely self-destructive spiral for her. Over the next few weeks, she turned into what seemed like a wild animal. She became extremely belligerent, defiant, and spun completely out of control. She would sneak out of the house and stay out all night. She always called to let me know that she was okay but that she was not coming home. She would not divulge her whereabouts or whom she was with. She stole my ATM card and knew the pin number, and she withdrew several hundred dollars out of my account. When she would return home, she was obviously high and didn't care. It was as if she was doing everything she could to end up either in jail or dead. She stated that she didn't care about anything or anybody. Getting high was her escape, and the more she did it, the more she enjoyed the feeling that nothing matters. She said, "Since everyone thinks I'm such a bad kid and a loser, that's what I'll be."

By now, I was seriously ill – physically, emotionally, and spiritually. I felt completely lost and didn't know where to turn. Jim had pretty much thrown up his hands in complete disgust and decided he had to get away from the day-to-day turmoil of our lives. He just couldn't deal with it, and he couldn't help Kristin or me because he was lost in grief, anger, and resentment. While I couldn't comprehend then how he could just walk out and leave me and our daughters in the state we were in, intellectually I understood it. We needed a time out – our relationship had become unhealthy for our kids and for us. In retrospect, his leaving probably saved our marriage. But it would take a long time for me to forgive him and for me let go of my own anger and resentment toward him. On the day he left, the raw sewage overflowing in the toilets and bathtubs from our septic tank problem could not have been a more graphic representation of my feelings. And it was about to get even worse before I made the decision to take some drastic measures to save Kristin and myself.

CHAPTER SEVENTEEN

An Out of Control Adolescent

Within 72 hours of Jim's departure, it was as if my whole world was caving in rapidly. Kristin was out of control, and I actually thought that she had become psychotic. I couldn't eat, think clearly, or sleep, and my normal 112-pound body now weighed in at 100 pounds. My clothes literally just hung on me. Our finances were in disarray, as the market had crashed and many of our investments had gone south. I was angry at everyone, including God. I definitely was playing the pitiful victim role. It was the beginning of my continuous thoughts that I was in a deep dark hole with no way out and that falling asleep and never waking up would be easier than facing the reality of what my life had become. I began thinking of suicide constantly.

The substance-abuse psychologist who had been treating Kristin felt that she had reached a point of no return and, unless I took some drastic measures, she was heading for catastrophe. I began calling in-patient adolescent-drug-abuse programs that my insurance company had recommended and discovered that these programs are all voluntary, meaning that my child would have to recognize that she had a problem and want help. This was a major predicament, as Kristin did not feel she had a problem and did not want help. She was not going to *volunteer* to go anywhere. Out of complete frustration, I turned to the Internet and began doing extensive research on struggling teens. I was overwhelmed with the amount of information on the Web. I discovered a vast array of programs ranging from boot camps to therapeutic boarding schools to long-term residential treatment programs to wilderness programs. I must have spent a complete 24 hours glued to my computer reading about these programs and must have made more than 50 phone calls talking to various professionals about my daughter's situation. The consistent message I heard from all of them was that I needed to get my daughter out of her current environment. The fact that she felt she had no problem was a common trait among the teenagers who attended these programs. I was shocked at the amount of money these programs cost, ranging from $50,000 to $100,000 per year, and most insurance companies did not cover them. I called my insurance company and found that none of these programs would be covered under my benefits plan.

I stumbled across a boarding school in northern Connecticut that had an education philosophy of character building. I talked to the admissions director and really liked their program. The kids who attended this school were all teenagers like Kristin. Most had past problems of substance abuse, defiance, low self-esteem, and poor academic achievement. They accepted kids to the program based on the child's willingness to want to change the destructive path they were on. I was informed that Kristin and I would have to come in for an extensive interview.

I talked to Kristin about the school and told her it could be a fresh start for her. She agreed to go to the interview but was emphatic that there was nothing wrong with her and that she didn't need to change anything about herself. Nevertheless, she made the four-hour drive with me to attend the interview, albeit practically kicking and screaming. As soon as we arrived on campus, she immediately said, "There's no way I'm going to school here. It looks like a prison."

"Don't be so quick to make a judgment based on the physical appearance of the school," I told her. "Just have an open mind." I must admit, aesthetically, the school did not look that appealing, but we were not there for aesthetics.

We talked to the admissions director, going through the background and history of how we got to where we were with Kristin. We then toured the school, and I could tell by Kristin's body language that she hated it. We then went through an intensive interview with several staff members, and Kristin proceeded to show her defiance and her negative attitude. She stated, "I don't want to come here to school. There's nothing wrong with me. I like smoking pot, and there's nothing wrong with it. I don't need to change anything about myself."

After a few hours of this type of dialogue, the admissions director spoke to me alone. He said, "We could really help your daughter, but she's not ready for our school. We can't accept her to our program because she has not accepted that she has a need to change." He went on to tell me that many kids like my daughter do well in their program after attending a wilderness program. He highly recommended that I send her to such a program, and he gave me the names of several that he felt were the most successful. He wished me luck and told me that they would be glad to interview my daughter again if she had a change of heart. I left the school with Kristin feeling defeated and frustrated once again.

The drive back home seemed to take forever. I told Kristin that we could not continue to go down this path – that something had to change. Her response was, "If everyone would just leave me alone and stay out of my life, I would be fine." I told her that she was in deep denial, and if she continued she was going to end up dead or in jail. She said, "You don't know anything, Mom, Just leave me alone." We sat in complete silence for the rest of the car ride. I felt weak and nauseous and was silently praying for God to give me the strength to drive us back home safely. Once we arrived home, I got in my bed and cried myself to sleep. I slept for about two hours and woke up to find that Kristin was not home. I knew that when she returned, she would be stoned, as this had become the story of our lives for the past few weeks. As if to insure that she met my expectations, she returned home later that night stoned out of her mind and went into her room, blasting her stereo so loud that the base of the music was bouncing off of the walls.

The events of the next evening are what put me over the edge and caused me to do the unthinkable – call the police on my own daughter. I had been in bed for most of the day, as by now my blood count was so severely low that I had no energy and was completely lethargic. Kristin was blasting her stereo, and I went to her room to tell her to turn it down. As I entered the hallway leading to her room, the smell of marijuana hit me like a slap in the face. I banged on her bedroom door and screamed at her to let me in. She opened the door, and her room was filled with marijuana smoke. I said, "Are you out of your mind sitting in this room smoking pot?"

"Mom, you don't know what you're talking about. You don't even know what pot smells like. I'm not doing anything," she said.

I replied, "Do you think I'm an idiot? I know what pot smells like. You are high out of your mind."

"Get the hell out of my room mom. Get out of my life and leave me the fuck alone."

Strictly on impulse, I slapped her face and said, "Don't you ever talk to me that way, young lady." I then resorted to a phrase my mom had used on me a couple of times when I was a teenager. I said, "I brought you into this world, and I will take you out. You will not disrespect me."

She responded with a scary rage in her eyes, "You fucking bitch, I hate you," and she threw the remote control of her stereo at me, barely missing my head. I went over and grabbed a small box sitting on her nightstand, which I suspected contained her stash of pot.

She grabbed my arm and yelled, "Don't touch that! It's mine! Get the fuck out of here!"

With that, we actually began wrestling with each other, as I tried to take the box and she violently tried to keep it from me. I could not believe that that I was on the ground in a physical battle with my 14-year-old daughter. We were both yelling and screaming and crying.

Jennifer heard the commotion and ran upstairs to find me and her sister on the ground fighting like mud wrestlers. She screamed at her sister, "Stop it! Leave Mom alone! You're hurting her!"

I yelled to Jennifer, "Help me get the box out of Kristin's hand!" Before I knew it, Jennifer grabbed her sister, who was now sitting on top of me, and threw her across the room. I opened the box, and, as I suspected, it contained a large stash of marijuana. I ran to the bathroom with Kristin chasing me and flushed it down the toilet.

She screamed, "No, no! Don't do that! I need that!" She then proceeded to go into what seemed like a psychotic tirade, throwing and breaking everything in her sight.

I kept yelling, "Stop! You're out of control – this has gone too far! You need help. Let me take you to the hospital so we can get you the help you need."

By now she was like a maniac running around the house screaming obscenities and destroying everything she could get her hands on. Jennifer was crying hysterically and pleading with me to call the police.

She said, "Mom, she's gone crazy. She's going to kill us."

I told Kristin, "If you don't stop right now and calm down, you leave me no choice but to call the police."

"Call the fucking pigs, you bitch. They're not going to do anything," she said, as she threw a crystal vase across the room and it shattered into a million small pieces of glass.

I knew we were at the point of no return, and I honestly feared for all of our safety. I picked up the phone and dialed 911. I said to the dispatcher, "I need help. I have an out of control 14-year-old daughter who has a drug problem, and I need help to get her to a hospital." I knew I was walking a fine line, as I did not divulge that I had found marijuana and flushed it down the toilet. I did not want Kristin to get arrested; I wanted to get her help.

Within five minutes, two squad cars and the rescue squad arrived. Kristin by now had calmed down and was sitting on the couch in our basement as if nothing had happened. I told the police that my daughter was obviously high and that she had become uncontrollable and I just wanted to get her to the hospital. I had four officers and two paramedics in my home. Two of the officers and the paramedics went downstairs to talk to Kristin while the other two officers asked if they could look in her room. I gave them permission to search her room but made it clear that I was not calling to have my daughter arrested; I just wanted to get her to the hospital. After the officers and the paramedics spent about 30 minutes talking to Kristin, I was flabbergasted by what they told me.

"Mrs. Whaley, unfortunately, there's nothing we can do. If we had found drugs in your daughter's possession, we could arrest her and take her to Juvenile. However, for us to take her to the hospital, we would have to ask that she be committed to the psychiatric ward. Since your daughter states that she is not going to harm herself or anyone in the house and she is not in a psychotic state that we have witnessed, we can't have her committed. The hospital would just send her back home. We're sorry, this must be very frustrating for you."

I said, "I can't believe this. It just gives my daughter more validation that she's untouchable."

One of the officers suggested that if I felt I could no longer handle my daughter, I could call Children and Family Services and petition to have her turned over to the courts. He warned me that if I made that decision, once she was in the system, it would be hard to get her out. I would basically be relinquishing my parental rights.

The officers and paramedics left my home, and I felt completely helpless. Kristin came upstairs and simply said, "I told you they wouldn't do anything." I just looked at her in disgust as tears rolled down my face. She stared back at me with a kind of sadness in her eyes that was almost pleading for understanding and help. As much as she was in denial about her issues, I knew that she knew life had to change. She went to her room, and I could hear her sobbing. Jennifer gave me a hug and said, "Mom, I love you. It's going to be okay." And there I stood, in the middle of the kitchen, feeling worn, torn, physically and emotionally weak, and in despair as I sobbed in Jennifer's arms. She comforted me, as if she was the mother and I was the child.

I went to my bedroom and called Jim in Atlanta and gave him the news of this latest turn of events. The conversation only upset me more. It actually infuriated me, as his comment was, "I don't know what to tell you – put her out of the house."

"Jim, she's 14. I can't just put her out on the streets."

"Fine then – do what you want, but don't bother me with this bullshit. I don't care what you do with her."

I hung up on him and hated him at that moment. I thought to myself, *what an insensitive bastard I'm married to.*

I knelt by my bed and started praying out loud to God. I said, "God, please give me a sign of what to do. I don't have the answers, but I know that you do. God, I'm putting all of my trust in you. And whatever your will is, let it be done." I got in bed, but I couldn't sleep. I tossed and turned for hours. And then, as I lay on my back looking up at the ceiling, I noticed a shadow in the shape of an arrow, but I couldn't tell where the shadow was coming from. I took it as a sign from God that I had to move forward. That I had to stop wallowing in self-pity and defeat. That I couldn't sit around and waste away waiting for my husband to come back and rescue Kristin and me. I made up my mind that first thing in the morning, I would call the wilderness program, Redcliff Ascent, and make arrangements for Kristin go there. I decided on Redcliff because it was the program that kept coming to mind – as if God had planted the seed that it was the right place for Kristin. I felt clarity and at peace. I closed my eyes and fell asleep and slept better than I had slept in weeks.

The next morning, I made the phone call to Redcliff Ascent and engaged in the admissions process for Kristin. I was convinced that my choices were limited. I could let her continue to self-destruct, I could turn her over to the courts, or I could pay a hefty price for her to be in a private program away from her existing environment. At that point, the costs didn't matter, as my child's life was priceless to me. My fax machine stayed busy all morning with the multitude of forms that needed to be completed and faxed back. I knew that there was no way Kristin would willingly get on an airplane with me to go to Utah to attend a therapeutic wilderness program. And I knew that if she even had an inkling that I was sending her away, she would run away from home. I was advised that most kids get to the program with the help of a youth escort service. This whole concept of hiring someone to fly in and practically kidnap my child in the middle of the night was a scary thought to me. But after speaking to several references who had used the youth escort service I was considering, I was convinced it was the only way I could get Kristin to Utah. I put all of my faith and trust in God that I was doing the right thing. I made the decision to send her away, and there was no turning back.

I made all the necessary arrangements, and the escort service was to arrive two days later on September 21, 2002, at 5:30 AM. Kristin would need to take nothing with her. I was told that the average length of stay in the wilderness program was 60 days, but some kids required less time and some kids required more. I was told that my only contact with my daughter would be via letters, but every week there would be a call between me and the staff to discuss her progress. I was warned that I would initially receive heart-wrenching letters from Kristin informing me that she was being abused and to come get her. The program is completely outdoors, and the kids are provided only the necessities for survival. There are no outside distractions of common everyday life, such as TV, computers, or CD players. The child has no choice but to eventually come to terms with his or her issues and deal with them head on.

I called Jim and informed him of my decision. His initial reaction was, "Are you out of your mind? We can't afford it."

I told him, "We can't afford not to do this. If I do nothing and she ends up dead, I won't be able to live with myself."

I gave him the Web address so he could view the site and get more information about the program and where she was going. He said, I'll look at the Web site and call you later."

I then called my mother and both of my sisters. They had no idea how bad things had gotten. They all supported me and my decision and told me I was doing the right thing. They all prayed with me and told me to keep trusting and believing that God would see me through this. Jim called me later that day after viewing the Web site, and while he was skeptical that this was the right thing to do, he was supportive. In all honesty, it didn't matter to me at that point what he thought, as I felt he had abandoned us and I was now consciously making unilateral decisions in the best interest of our child. As far as I was concerned, Jim and I were heading to divorce court.

Amazingly, over the next two days, while Kristin had no clue what was about to happen, she said all the right things and her behavior was almost angelic. She told me how sorry she was for how she had acted. She said she knew that she had some serious issues and she wanted to do better, but it was so hard. She said, "Mom, I just feel stuck. It's hard to get out of what I've gotten myself into. You can't possibly understand." I started to second-guess myself, and for a quick second, I thought about backing out of sending her away. But I had heard all these words before from her, and I knew that changing my plans would be a mistake. We had two great days together, and I purposely kept her busy to ensure she didn't sneak out of the house and disappear. On her last night at home before she was to be taken away, I cooked a big dinner and Kristin, Jennifer, and I sat and ate, talking and laughing almost like old times. Neither of them seemed fazed by their father's separation from us. It was as if they both silently understood him, and they both knew he just needed time away and would be back.

I had already explained in private to Jennifer what was going to happen with Kristin. I showed her a videotape about the program, and she said, "Mom, this will be good for her. You're doing the right thing." I told her that when the escort service came, her sister probably would cause a big scene and to just stay in her room. She promised me she would. She hugged me and comforted me, saying, "I love you. Everything is going to be okay." I told her how proud I was of her and how much I loved her. For I knew that, in many ways, she had become an innocent victim of this chaotic life we had been living for the past year. I was amazed at her maturity and how she seemed to be the most levelheaded person in our entire family. She had become a pillar of strength for me and was literally taking care of me on many levels. She knew I was not well, and she was very concerned about how thin I had become. She would constantly tell me, "Mom, you have to eat. You're becoming a skeleton."

At 10:00 PM on September 20, the phone rang, and I immediately picked it up, as I was expecting a call from the escort service informing me that their flight had arrived. I informed them that things were rather calm with Kristin and that I would be on the lookout for them at 5:30 AM. I then asked, "What happens if she refuses to go with you?" They assured me that she would go and that, even if she initially put up a fight, she would go willingly. I hung up the phone and once again talked out loud to God asking him to give me the strength and courage to go through with this. I was stepping out completely on faith. After all, I had already signed a power of attorney giving the escort service temporary custody of Kristin, allowing them to transport her across state lines. I was literally entrusting my daughter to strangers.

I went into Kristin's room, and she was lying across her bed reading a magazine. I asked her if she wanted a back massage – something she loves and I knew wouldn't turn down. She said, "Okay, Mom, but don't do one of those quickie massages. Do it for a long time."

"I'll do it for as long as you want," I said.

As I massaged her back, I said, "You know how much I love you, right?"

"I know you love me, Mom."

"And your dad loves you too."

"I know he does."

I then went on to tell her that no matter happened in her life to always know that she is loved and that I would never do anything to hurt her. I told her that I would give my life for her and to always remember that no matter what.

She said, "Mom, what's wrong with you? Are you dying or something?"

I was trying so hard to fight back the tears, but I couldn't. I told her between my sobs, "No, I'm not dying. I just love you so much, and I just want you to be okay. Just promise me that you will always remember how much I love you no matter what happens."

She said, "I promise." She turned over and sat up and wiped my tears from my face. She reached out for me with her arms, and we sat in a tight emotional embrace and both wept. I was crying because I knew it would be the last time I would hold her in my arms for a long time. She was crying because I think she genuinely wanted to end her pain and mine. I kissed her goodnight, left her room, and went across the hall to kiss Jennifer goodnight.

I knew I would not get any sleep that night, so I planned to just stay awake. I also wanted to ensure that Kristin did not attempt to sneak out of the house, something she had become accustomed to doing over the preceding months. It was now almost midnight, and I tried to keep my mind occupied by reading a book. I heard Kristin's bedroom door open, and I bolted up thinking she was trying to leave the house. But I was surprised to find that it was Jennifer who had entered her sister's bedroom. I stood in the hallway and could hear Jennifer say to her sister, "Are you asleep?"

"No," Kristin responded.

"I just wanted to say goodnight and tell you I love you," Jennifer said.

"I love you too. But why are you and Mom acting so weird?"

"We're not acting weird. You just should know how much we love you."

"Okay, I feel the love. I want to get some sleep," Kristin replied. I went back to my bedroom, as I did not want to intrude on this special moment Jennifer had shared with Kristin. I knew it was her way of saying goodbye to her big sister.

At 1:00 AM, the phone rang, startling me. I picked up, and it was Jim. "Lisa, are you still proceeding with the plans?" he asked.

"Yes," I responded.

"Do you think Kristin has any idea what's going on?"

"No, I don't think so."

"Listen, I love you and I love the girls. I'm sorry I'm not there with you and you're going through this alone. But I do love you."

"Jim, I love you too."

"Call me after Kristin leaves. I know this is hard, and I do think you're doing the right thing."

With that we said goodnight.

The next four and a half hours seemed to take forever to go by. I was reading a book called *Miracles Happen When Women Pray*. But I couldn't concentrate and found myself reading the same page over and over. I turned the TV on and flipped through the channels, but nothing held my attention. I went into the laundry room and proceeded to fold some clothes that had been left in the dryer. I was clearly trying to find something, anything, to do that would make the time pass quickly and keep me occupied. It was now 3:00 AM, and my anxiety and adrenalin were at an all-time high. I went up to Kristin's room and quietly opened the door to look in on her the way I used to when she was a small child. She looked so sweet and innocent lying there asleep. I stood there for about ten minutes just watching her and listening to her breathe. I had this sudden urge to crawl in bed with her and hold her in my arms but was fearful that she might wake up and find it rather odd that I was in bed with her. I walked over and stroked her hair as she slept. She had that same look of perfect beauty that she had when she was born. I couldn't help but think of Stevie Wonder's song "Isn't She Lovely," which played on the radio the day we drove home from the hospital after she was born. That was such a magical moment in our lives, filled with so much happiness, hope, and promise. Here we were 14 years later, and in two and a half hours she would be awakened by two strangers who would take her away. It was almost incomprehensible to me – but it was reality.

Those last two and half hours went by fast, as I must have dozed off lying on the couch in our family room. The sound of a car coming down our driveway woke me up. I quickly got up and put our three dogs in the basement so they wouldn't bark. My heart was beating so fast, and I thought I was going to hyperventilate. This was the moment of truth for me. Could I actually go through with this? I opened the front door to greet the male and female from the escort service before they even knocked. The male was quite large and looked like a bodybuilder. The female was average size, but she looked like she was in great physical shape. They were both extremely kind and professional. We went into the kitchen, and I signed some final documents and we went over the procedures. I was to enter Kristin's room with the male and female and wake her up. I was to tell her that I loved her but it was time for her to deal with her issues, so I was sending her to Utah to attend Redcliff Ascent's Therapeutic Wilderness Program so she could receive the help that she needed. I was to tell her that I wanted her to cooperate with the people there who were going to escort her to Utah. I was then to leave the room, go to my room, and not come back out, leaving the rest up to the escort service. I was instructed that no matter what happened, I was not to come back out of my room until they were gone. The escort service assured me that my daughter was going to be fine and that they were professionals and would take great care of her and get her to Utah without incident. They promised to call me as soon as they arrived at the airport. They both gave me a hug and said, "This is probably the hardest thing you've ever had to do, but trust us, it will be fine." They then said, "Are you ready Mrs. Whaley?"

"Yes. Let's just get his over with before I change my mind."

We walked upstairs and entered Kristin's room. I woke her up and as soon as she saw those two people standing by her bed with me, it was as if she knew she was being taken away. She said, "Get the fuck out of my room." I went through the dialogue as I had been instructed and left her room. I went into my bedroom and stood by the door trying to listen to every word being said. Surprisingly, Kristin did not put up too big of a big fuss. I heard her say, "I'm not going anywhere with you."

I heard the male say, "Actually you are. You have two choices. I will leave the room, but she (the female) will stay in here with you so you can put some clothes on. Or, I can pick you up and wrap you in that blanket and take you as you are. Those are your only two choices. So which is it going to be?"

"Fine then. Just get out so I can get dressed."

I heard the male come out of her room and close the door as he stood by it. A few minutes later, I heard him knock on her door and say, "You have 30 seconds."

Then I heard, "You have 15 seconds."

And then, "I'm coming in."

I heard her door open, and then I heard Kristin say, "What about all my stuff? I need to pack some clothes."

"No, you don't need to take anything with you. Everything you need will be provided for you."

I heard them walk downstairs, and one of the escorts must have touched Kristin's arm, as I heard her say, "Don't fucking touch me. I can walk by myself."

As they were walking out of the front door, Kristin yelled, "Bye, Mom. Have a nice life."

I stood watching from my bedroom window as they got in the car. I was sobbing uncontrollably. That look on her face of an almost angelic quality is etched in my memory forever. She actually looked relieved, like she knew she was finally being rescued from her own living hell. I watched the car drive down our long driveway, and I put my hand on the windowpane as if to try to touch her. I whispered her name and said, "Goodbye, Kristin. I love you so much. God, please go with her and take care of her. I'm leaving her in your hands."

I thought this was the end of the long treacherous journey with Kristin, but it was really just the beginning of the long healing process that would be necessary for all of us to rebuild our lives. When she left, I expected that she would return to me in 60 days at a cost of $30,000. But I was wrong – it would take much longer. She spent 72 days in the wilderness and then had a brief stay at Mt. Bachelor Academy, a therapeutic boarding school in Oregon, which she ran away from on Christmas day. She returned to the wilderness for another 40 days and then spent 6 months at Logan River Academy, a residential treatment center in Logan, Utah. In total, it was 10 months and $100,000 before Kristin returned home. I knew I had done the right thing when she told me in a letter she wrote, "Mom, you saved my life. If you wouldn't have sent me away, I know I would have ended up dead. Thank you for not giving up on me."

Yes, her life was priceless to me, and I would have given my own life to save hers – and I almost did.

CHAPTER EIGHTEEN

The Process of Reclaiming My Soul

After I sent Kristin away, I finally could focus on my own issues. I had been so consumed with trying to save her that I had been existing on adrenalin and nothing more. I had ignored my own physical, emotional, and spiritual issues. I had so many life-changing decisions to make. I really thought that my marriage was over, and I needed to start making preparations for life without Jim, physically, emotionally and financially. It was hard for me to imagine life without him. He was my soul mate, and I loved him unconditionally. I knew he was suffering with his own issues, and I worried about him more than I worried about myself. I was very worried about Jennifer, as she has always been introverted and I knew she was internalizing all that had happened. I knew that she too was hurting, but she never wanted to talk much about what was going on or how she was feeling. She would just say, "Mom, don't worry about me. I'm fine."

In the week that followed after Kristin was gone, it seemed that every day there was more bad news. We were behind on our taxes, and the IRS wanted to be paid a substantial amount of money, including penalties and interest. Jennifer's final tuition payment for her private school was due. We had property taxes due. It seemed like everything was due all at the same time. I had just shelled out $30,000 for payment to Redcliff Ascent, and our funds were depleting rapidly. I was doing some serious creative financial management, moving funds around and pretty much using the "rob Peter to pay Paul" method at times while I liquidated assets. I was completely overwhelmed and more and more saw no way out.

I became incapable of working, as I was so distracted by the events of my life, as well as incapacitated by my physical and mental illnesses. I was in no condition to manage people or make business decisions. Intellectually, I knew that I was sinking into a deep and dangerous depression. I didn't want to accept it, though. After all, how could I, the always smiling and bubbly Lisa, be depressed? The girl who always had it together and had it all, according to everyone else's perception. I was so disgusted and embarrassed by my situation. I was ashamed. More and more, I just didn't want to cope or deal with life. More and more, I disconnected from friends and family. I didn't want to talk to anyone. It was too hard to pretend that everything was fine. I was tired of pretending. I was tired of the façade.

And then I realized that I had made an assumption that Kristin would only need to be away for 60 days. What if she needed to be away longer? How was I going to pay for it? I saw no upside to anything. I was tired, I was weak, and I was weary. I pulled out my life insurance policy and looked it over carefully. I calculated my IBM pension and the survivor benefits that Jim would receive if I died. It seemed that my death would be a blessing. I would be out of my misery, and Jim would have enough funds to ensure that Kristin got the care she needed for as long as she needed. I knew that he would take great care of our kids because, despite all that had happened, he was a great father and he genuinely loved his children, and they loved him. There would be enough insurance money to ensure that our kids could continue to be provided for in the lifestyle that they were accustomed to. I had made up my mind; I would take my own life and put myself out of my wretchedness.

On the morning that that I sat in my car in the closed garage with the engine running, it's the most cowardly and selfish thing I've ever done in my life. It would have been the easy way out for me, but it would have torn apart my loved ones' lives. It would have destroyed my children's world, as they would have to go through the rest of their lives carrying the burden that their own mother had killed herself. It would have been an unforgivable act of self-indulgence. I thank God every day that I did not go through with it and that I came to my senses and asked for help. It was indeed the day that I realized my *soul* was in the lost and found, and it was the day I decided to go back and reclaim it.

I took a medical leave of absence from work and began my passage of healing and self-discovery. As part of the process of reclaiming my soul, I began reevaluating every dimension and crevice of my life. I started thinking about the fact that, even before "the perfect storm," when things were relatively good in my life, I often felt unfulfilled. I often felt that even with everything I had and all that I had accomplished, something was missing in my life. And something was indeed missing – my spirituality. I had stopped going to church, and I had become isolated from the very spiritual beliefs that I had been raised with. In some ways, perhaps I thought I was bigger than God, that I didn't need him. My mom had often told me over the years that sometimes we get so high and mighty that we

217

think we don't need God. But he will knock us down off of our high horse so fast that we won't know what hit us. I wondered if that's what God had done to me. I needed him in my life more than ever, and I was ready to commit my life to him.

I set up an appointment with the Reverend Dr. Charles Ferrara, Pastor Chuck, as he's called, the minister of the church I had briefly attended when we first moved to Connecticut. What an astonishing man of God he is. I opened up and talked to him as if I had known him my entire life. He had such a way with words and such a calming effect to his voice. There were so many similarities in our lives. He also had two daughters, both adults now. Our younger daughters both were named Jennifer. His older daughter's name was Christina, similar to Kristin. His children were also multiracial, for his wife of over 30 years was Korean. He was once a New York City police officer, so this was a man who had seen a lot in his lifetime. He prayed with me, and he talked openly with me, sharing some of his own personal experiences. I told him that I felt like God had something he wanted me to do, but I wasn't sure what it was. I told him that I knew I had been blessed with so many gifts and talents, and I wanted to find a way to use those gifts and talents for the Lord. I talked about my love and passion for public speaking and my love of writing. I told him how ashamed I was that I had considered taking my own life, that I was so embarrassed by the recent events of my life. He told me that I should not be ashamed or embarrassed and that I was not alone; so many people have gone through similar events in their lives. He told me that it was obvious that I was a great leader and that people looked up to me and were drawn to me. Perhaps God wanted me to use my gifts of speaking and writing to share my experiences with others. It was this conversation with Pastor Chuck that gave me the inspiration to write this book. I felt certain that this is what God was calling me to do.

I also had a team of professionals who were instrumental in helping me through the process of reclaiming my soul. My physician put me through a battery of medical tests and finally got a conclusive diagnosis of the blood disorder that was causing my lack of energy, severe headaches, achy joints, and weight loss. With an assortment of medication, my physical ailments were quite treatable. My psychiatrist, Dr. Mark Ligorski, was wonderful and took great care to educate me about depression. I came to understand that depression is nothing to be ashamed of. It is a legitimate medical problem and can be serious if not treated. We went through the process of trying various medications to rectify the chemical imbalance in my brain. And then there was my therapist, Monique Goldman, an amazing woman who saw right through me from the moment we met and would not allow me to play the façade game that I had become a master at playing. We spent countless hours together over the next year dissecting every part of my life from childhood to the present time. I allowed her to get to know me more intimately than anyone had known me. I let my guard down completely with her and, for the first time in my life, divulged things I had carried around unexpressed for years. With her help, I engaged in the process of real self-discovery and self-acceptance. She too is a woman of great faith, and we often talked about the power of prayer. We talked about the importance of having mind, body, and soul all working in sync and how if either one of those components is ill, the total person will eventually break down. In my case, all three of those components were severely ill, causing me to crash and burn. She too was instrumental in encouraging me to write this book. If nothing more, it would be an excellent therapeutic exercise for

, the writing process, I learned more and more about myself. It

.n opportunity to truly reflect on my life, my successes and

some of the mistakes I made on my journey through time, and most importantly, all the many blessings and miracles I've witnessed in my life.

I began reconnecting with friends I had distanced myself from. I learned who my real friends were and who my acquaintances were. My real friends were there for me and didn't judge me. They listened, they cried with me, and they encouraged me. I think some were actually relieved to find out that I was a real person after all, flawed like everyone else, and not this perfect woman that they had perceived me to be or that I had perceived myself to be. I discovered who my real supporters at work were, who genuinely cared about me as an individual and not just as an IBM robot. There were a few significant people who I learned I could completely trust, and there were a few I trusted who let me down, betraying my trust. There were those who went out of their way to help me, and then there were those who were in a position to help but didn't.

I began to seriously evaluate my marriage, and despite all that had happened, I knew that I did not want it to end. I wanted to free myself of the hurt, anger, and resentment I felt and be at peace with myself and with Jim, whether we reconciled our marriage or not. I realized that I could not change Jim or anything that had happened. I could only change myself. Divorce, like suicide, seemed like a copout to me. It became evident to me that we sometimes marry accepting too little in the beginning and then expect too much in the end. When our expectations aren't met, we bail. We divorce and tear our families a part. It's a sad state of affairs in our society, with one out of two marriages ending in divorce. Marriage is hard work and perhaps, as a woman who was trying to have it all, I became like so many other women, delusional relative to my expectations of marriage.

Two of my friends from college, Marian and Marcia, had both attended a Women's Weekend retreat sponsored by The Sterling Institute of Relationship. I had recently reconnected with Marian and Marcia, and they both encouraged me to attend the weekend. They both told me what a wonderful experience it was for them and how it fundamentally changed their lives. They thought I would get a lot out it and actually be a great contributor. They both told me, "Lisa, you will come away from the weekend a more powerful woman than you already are." They told me to trust them, and I did. I attended the weekend, and it was life changing for me.

During my women's weekend experience, I got so much clarity about my life. I learned so much about myself and how I am in all of my relationships – with Jim, my daughters, my parents, my siblings, my friends, and my colleagues. The weekend is run by A. Justin Sterling and was started over 20 years ago as the result of a professional relationship he developed with the director of a women's organization that counseled women about how to be successful in their careers. They began to see a correlation between women's ability to be successful in their careers and their inability to be successful in their personal relationships. The essential core of the philosophy Sterling teaches during the weekend is that "men and women are different on many different levels – biological, psychological, intellectual, emotional. Even though in the past 30 years the popular culture has tended to ignore those differences, men and women should embrace those qualities that make them intrinsically male and intrinsically female." The relationship model the weekend encourages both men and women to adopt is: "One which is predicated upon defining the differences between men and women; and identifying, embracing, and projecting those differences into the relationship. As men and women begin to understand

and accept their differences, they can begin to respect and accept each other in a successful long-term relationship that is based on celebrating those differences rather than trying to become more like each other."

The basic philosophy of the Women's Weekend is that "when a woman begins to accept and embrace all of her female characteristics, then she can make wise choices. These choices are very personal ones, ones that will affect the direction and outcome of the rest of her life. A woman's freedom lies in the acceptance of her feminine nature, not in trying to adopt what are fundamentally male characteristics. While many people may find this philosophy controversial or a throwback to the 50s, "it's really about accepting, respecting, and honoring biology, psychology, and evolution." The Sterling philosophy offers both men and women a choice – a choice to see relationships in a different way; a choice to try something that has worked for thousands of people who have utilized the philosophy and techniques.

I became a believer is Sterling's philosophy and adopted many of his relationship techniques in all of my day-to-day relationships. I was amazed at what a difference it made and witnessed positive transformations in all of my relationships. My weekend experience was a significant event in my journey to reclaim my soul.

As I reclaimed my soul, I found that fighting spirit in me once again. Instead of focusing on all of the things that were wrong in my life, I began focusing on all of the things that were right. I started counting my blessings that I did have choices that I could make and, while they were difficult choices, making them would allow me to once again to gain harmony in my life. I realized that my life would be whatever I perceived it to be. I thought about something I had heard Anthony Robbins say years ago that stuck with me like glue: "People don't get what they want out of life because they simply fail to take action." I went into action mode, as I was tired of sitting on the sidelines watching life pass me by. I wanted to get back in the game and play ball – not just watch the game from the bleachers. I wrote out an extensive list of things that I wanted to change about my life. I identified the barriers that were in my way and put an action plan together of how I was going to get around the barriers and accomplish the things I wanted to accomplish. I had target dates and milestones, and it became my personal roadmap for my journey.

I got rid of some of my financial pressures by ridding myself of material luxuries that weren't necessary. I sold our Mercedes SL500 Sports Convertible, an expensive luxury that sat parked in the garage five months out of the year. I sold my Mercedes ES430, as it was the car I almost took my own life in and every time I sat in it, I got cold chills. I bought a less expensive and more practical Mercedes SUV, a great vehicle for dealing with the winter snow in Connecticut.

After talking to numerous professionals about my long battle with the public school Kristin had attended, I became more convinced that the school had failed her as much as I had. After thoroughly reviewing every detail of her school records, it was blatantly obvious that there were numerous red flags that she was at great risk academically and emotionally before she ever got in trouble with drugs. Yet the school did nothing, even after my numerous meetings and requests for her to be tested. I felt her civil rights had been violated. I hired an educational attorney that our juvenile attorney recommended. I took legal action against the Board of Education, and we reached an amicable resolution.

I met with a team of HR and Occupational Health executives at IBM and shared with them the financial impact of my daughter's care and my frustration with lack of insurance coverage for her care. While our IBM benefits are some of the best in the industry, I identified significant gaps in coverage when dealing with a teen in crisis and made several recommendations for ways to close the gap. If nothing more, I wanted to raise the executives' awareness of the problem in hopes of consideration for changes when our benefits were reevaluated.

And then, as I cleaned out my file cabinet at home one evening, I came across a document I had written several years before that contained my 10 guiding principles to finding synergy and harmony between life and work. As I read the document, it was an epiphany for me, as I realized that I had violated many of my own principles. I had written these principles after being asked numerous times by women I mentored inside and outside of IBM, "How do you do it? How do you make it work – the great career, the marriage, the kids, the flawless appearance? You make it look so easy." Obviously, looks can be deceiving, but I came up with 10 principles that I really tried to live my life by. Ironically, as I reflected back over these principles, I found that when I followed my principles, things in my life and at work were harmonious. It's when I strayed from them that I lost the synergy between life and work.

I abandoned the idea of work/life balance years ago after I became a manager. To me, balance implies things being equal. If you think of a set of scales with one side as life and the other side as work, it was obvious to me very early on in my career that I may never have *balance* between my life and work scales – but that was okay. It was more important to me that life and work was synchronized and that they worked together *synergistically* and *harmoniously*. I made conscientious choices at times that one, life or work, was going to take a back seat to the other. If my scales were tilted in either direction, I was okay with that. As long as I recognized the sacrifices that I was making in my life/work combination and I was okay with those sacrifices and choices, the equation worked fine. I got into trouble when I lost sight of my personal values and principles and allowed other people or circumstances to make choices for me. Over time, I became a creation of everyone else's image of me, and I got lost in that creation. I had clearly begun to live my life not by my own standards, but by what I perceived other people's standards to be for me. The resulting consequences were significantly dangerous.

Finally, in June of 2003, I was ready to return to work, but not in the same capacity as when I left. I asked to step out of my executive role and return in a part-time capacity that would still allow me to contribute to the business but with less pressure and stress. At that particular point in my life, it was the best thing for me and for IBM. Like so many other times in my IBM career, I had an abundance of support and was blessed that IBM was able to honor my request. We found a part-time role for me that allowed me to use my skills and add value to the business while keeping my life and work in harmony. I vowed to myself as I returned to work that I would live and work by my guiding principles. I would never again allow my identity to be defined by my work. I had my soul back, and I was determined to keep it!

CHAPTER NINETEEN

10 Guiding Principles to Finding Synergy and Harmony between Life and Work

In this chapter, I will discuss the 10 guiding principles to finding synergy and harmony between life and work. When I developed these principles, I developed them with women in mind. However, these same principles can be applied to men as well. The principles may seem quite simple and commonsensical, but I can attest to the fact that if you follow them and apply them to your own life and situation, they work. I will discuss each principle individually, giving specific examples of how I applied them.

1. Be yourself – don't try to be someone that you're not.
2. Set realistic goals for yourself that aren't in conflict with your personal values.
3. Be confident on the outside even though you may not be on the inside.

4. **Be passionate about what you do in your work life and your personal life.**

5. **Take charge of and responsibility for your own career and your own life.**

6. **Develop marketable skills that are valued inside and outside of your workplace.**

7. **Have a support network and use it.**

8. **Make time for yourself.**

9. **Celebrate successes and learn from failures.**

10. **Enjoy life. Have fun. Tomorrow isn't promised to you.**

1. <u>**Be yourself – don't try to be someone that you're not.**</u>

As I advanced in my career, I watched other female managers and executives inside and outside of IBM carefully. Some I looked up to and admired a great deal. But there were many that I vowed I would never want to be like, as they struck me as being more like men than like women in their demeanor, their appearance, the way they spoke, and their attitudes. Many didn't strike me as being comfortable with their feminine qualities. Some may as well have been men with ovaries. I think many women have this perception of how they are *supposed* to be as they enter into management or the executive ranks versus just being *who they are*.

Throughout my career, I would often hear from men and women that I was different than most managers or executives. I was often told that I didn't look like or act like the typical executive. I was always perplexed as to what people meant by that. I never changed my personality to fit the stereotype of how people perceived an executive to be. I've always been bubbly and a fun-loving type of person – kind of a kid at heart. As I advanced in my career, I remained that way. I didn't change who I was to try to fit some superficial manager or executive mold. If being myself had been a roadblock to climbing the corporate ladder, then the climb would not have been worth it to me. I knew I was a little different from many of my colleagues, but I learned to use those differences to my advantage versus trying to change to be like the masses. This is who I was, and I wasn't going to try to be someone that I wasn't.

The underlying notion behind this principle is that we are each different and unique. The qualities that we were born with that form our basic personality are what make each of us special in our own way. Whoever you are, be that person and be at peace with yourself – you don't have to try to be someone else to be successful. Success is not dependent on who we are. It's what we do with who we are that matters and makes the difference. A quote I love by Peace Pilgrim, who was an American activist (1901- 81), is, "When you find peace within yourself, you become the kind of person who can live at peace with others."

2. Set realistic goals for yourself that aren't in conflict with your personal values.

The importance of setting goals for yourself and actually writing them down is imperative. Yet I am amazed at how many people never take the time to do this. I tell people I coach that going through life without concrete goals and action plans is like taking a cross-country drive in your car without a road map. How would you know where you're going? Or if you're off course or on a detour? As Lee Iacocca said, "The discipline of writing something down is the first step toward making it happen."

Not only is it essential that you set short-term and long-terms goals, but those goals should be realistic according to the type of life you want to lead and should not be in conflict with your personal values. This is a critical point, as it's so easy for us to set a goal for something that we *think* we want to achieve, but when we evaluate the sacrifices that may be necessary to achieve the goal, we often find that those sacrifices would be in conflict with our personal values. This would make the goal unrealistic. For example, certain jobs or positions do not lend themselves to a typical 9 to 5 workday. If you are a young woman with small children and your personal values are such that you desire to be home in the evenings with your children, then it might be unrealistic to have a goal to acquire a job or position that you know would require longer hours in the office. By doing so, you are setting yourself up for major conflict and disappointment. You would be compromising your personal values for the sake of the goal.

Writing the goal down is central because it makes it real – it's like making a commitment to yourself. When I started thinking about writing this book, I had many goals in my head relative to this project, but it wasn't until I actually wrote them down that I started taking action. With each goal, I set target dates and milestones. I developed an action plan with the steps I needed to take to achieve the goal. I kept the goals next to my computer so that everyday they were staring me in the face as if calling my name to work on them. Goals in your head can be somewhat like dreams or fantasies. Written goals are like staring at yourself in a mirror. They won't disappear – you can see them, you can touch them, and you can start working your plan to achieve them.

3. <u>Be confident on the outside even though you may not be on the inside.</u>

This is a principle that I adopted after hearing a female IBM senior executive whom I admired speak at an event I attended. She told a story about the time she was interviewing for a major position in IBM. That evening, after her interview, she talked to her husband and told him that she wasn't sure she was ready for this position. Maybe it was too big of a job for her. Maybe she wasn't ready for it. She went on to say that her husband asked her, "Do you think the men who are candidates for this job are at home telling their wives, 'Maybe I'm not ready for this job. Maybe it's too big of a job for me?" I loved this story because it drove home the point to me that, as women, we often doubt ourselves and our abilities. We are our own worst critics. Men don't seem to do this. Even if they aren't confident about their abilities, you would never know it. They have become masters at exuding confidence on the outside even though they may feel otherwise on the inside.

The executive's story really resonated with me. As I reflected back over my own career, I thought about each promotion I received and how I often doubted myself. I questioned my abilities and if I really was ready for each new responsibility that came with each promotion. However, my confidence characteristics were more male-like – I had become a master at exuding outward confidence even if I was extremely insecure internally. I really believe that this level of outward confidence in conjunction with my proven track record were key to several promotions I received.

But beware – being overly confident can work against you and cause you to be perceived as arrogant, egotistical, and self-righteous. The key to this confidence principle is to let it work in conjunction with Principle 1 – being yourself. If you are comfortable with who you are and you are comfortable with where you are relative to your skills and abilities, genuine confidence will develop over time almost naturally.

As William Shakespeare said, "Our doubts are traitors, and make us lose the good we oft might win by fearing to attempt."

4. **Be passionate about what you do in your work life and your personal life.**

If you aren't passionate about what do relative to your work or how you lead your life, then STOP – and start thinking about the fact that maybe it's time to do something different. Perhaps it's time to make some changes – minor or major ones. We are all naturally uncomfortable with change. It's much easier to go with the status quo than to go through the process of making changes in our work situation or life. There's nothing worse than waking up everyday hating what you do. With the amount of hours many of us put in at the office, we might as well enjoy what we do and be passionate about it. If not, it's a sure recipe to lead a miserable, unhappy, and unfulfilled existence.

Sure, we all have times when we have lows or may have the blues relative to our work or our life situation. But if you wake up day after day, week after week, and month after month hating your work or your life, you owe it to yourself and everyone around you to make some changes. Make no mistake, making changes in your work or life will not be easy, and it does take time. But doing *nothing* can be catastrophic in the long run.

When you have true passion for your work or how you lead your life, it becomes blatantly obvious to those around you. With passion comes enthusiasm and energy that's contagious. It's nearly impossible to be at your best and give your all to your work or your life when you're unhappy. It's easy to just go through the day-to-day motions of a mundane life. But who really wants to live that way? Do you?

Remember, "People don't get what they want out of life because they simply fail to take action." So be brutally honest with yourself – if you know you've lost that passion for the work that you do or the life that you are leading, then make a commitment to yourself right now to do something about it. Use Principle 2 – setting realistic goals. Start identifying the changes you want to make. Set short-term and long-term goals for yourself. Write them down and start building your action plan. After you do that, congratulations, for you've taken a big first step! But the hard work comes in *working your plan*. Trust me, anyone can do this. It just takes patience, determination, and a positive can-do attitude!

When I got my very first job with IBM as a programmer, I liked my job, but I knew I was never going to be passionate about it. I was being honest with myself. After two years, I knew it was time to make a change, and I was fully prepared to make whatever sacrifices were necessary to leave IBM if I had to in order to find work that I would be passionate about. It would have been easy to just continue to show up every day and not enjoy the work I was doing. But instead, I did something about it. I had the conversation with my manager about my desire to do something different. The rest is history. I'm amazed at how many people don't speak up for fear of being told no. Sometimes, we don't get what we want merely because we don't take the time to ask for it.

If this principle resonates with you, then what are you waiting for? *Get busy!*

5. <u>Take charge of and responsibility for your own life and your own career.</u>

This is the one principle that I violated miserably in the latter half of my career. While I did take responsibility for my own career, I allowed too many other people to exert their influence in making me believe that I wanted what they wanted for me. This was not intentional on anyone's part – it just happened. I caution people I coach to not to fall into this trap. You have to figure out what it is *you* want, otherwise other people who might have the best of intentions will try to figure it out for you.

Taking charge means being *proactive*, not just sitting around and waiting for things to magically happen for you or to you. It means not making excuses or rationalizing why things are or are not happening for you the way you'd like them to. Don't even attempt to apply this principle if you haven't applied Principle 2 – setting realistic goals. How can you take responsibility for and be in charge of *anything* if you don't even know what it is you're working toward?

When I was in a staff job earlier in my career, my kids were quite young, and I was struggling with synergizing life and work. I took responsibility for my life and career by coming up with an alternative work plan that allowed me to work from home two days a week. Even though my manager had discussed other alternatives, such as part-time work, I didn't settle for that alternative because I didn't think that it was in my best interest. Had I settled for his alternative, I would have been allowing him to take charge of my life and work situation. Instead, I came up with an alternative proposal that I felt would be better for me and the business and sold him on it. It was a win for both of us. I can't say it enough times – sometimes we don't get what we want merely because we don't take the time to ask for it.

When I was in the midst of "the perfect storm" of my life, it was easy for me to become a victim – and I did. The circumstances of my life had taken complete control over my mind, body, and soul. It would have been easy to quit and give up, as I almost did. But as soon as I took *charge of, and responsibility for* my life instead of making excuses and blaming everyone else, legitimately or not, things started to turn around for me. What a liberating feeling it is to stop allowing things to happen *to* you and start making things happen *for* you. When we are *persistent, believe* in ourselves, and are *consistent* in our efforts to make changes in our lives or work, we can accomplish things we never imagined possible.

6. Develop marketable skills that are valued inside and outside of your workplace.

Don't allow yourself to become a dinosaur! We all should be the constant student – always eager to learn and acquire new skills. We live in a fast-paced society that is dynamic and constantly changing. The most relevant skills desired in the marketplace evolve continuously. If you don't keep up and develop marketable skills, you will get left behind. You may wake up one day and find that your current skills aren't valued or necessary any longer in your current job. Where does that leave you if you have no marketable skills that the outside world values? Don't allow yourself to be caught in that position.

With every new position I ever achieved at IBM, I always asked myself two questions. First, what skills do I bring to the table that will allow me to add value and be successful in this position? Second, what new skills will I acquire that will be valuable inside and outside of IBM? As much as I love IBM and consider myself to be a loyal employee, I'm not so naive as to believe that I am above receiving a pink slip. It's about the needs of the business and, as much as laying people off is unpleasant; it's just a fact of the treacherous business climate most companies are faced with today. It's purely a fact of life. It's not personal – it's just business.

However, I've always tried to ensure that if I ever found myself in that unpleasant position, I would be ready by having marketable skills. I tell people I coach that the best time to look for a job is when you already have one. So don't allow yourself to become too comfortable or complacent. Be aware of what skills are desirable in the marketplace. Stay up-to-date with technology. READ, READ, READ! It's a great way to stay abreast of what's going on in the marketplace and where the jobs of the future are.

So ask yourself right now – do I have skills that are marketable inside and outside of my current workplace? If the answer is no, then do something about it. Use Principle 2 – setting realistic goals – and set a goal for yourself to acquire new skills. Then put your action plan together, and you know the most important step – *work your plan*!

7. <u>Have a support network and use it</u>.

I can't stress enough the magnitude of this principle in your work environment and in your life. Networking is a powerful tool. Those who have learned to use it effectively have a clear advantage. Always remember, you don't know what you don't know! The people you know also know people who know people. *What* you know is important, but *who* you know is equally important.

I tell people I coach that you can have great skills and abilities, but if the right people don't know who you are and what your skills and abilities are, you can go unnoticed. I've seen many smart, talented people go nowhere in their careers because they simply aren't visible to the right people.

Everyone should have a mentor, formally or informally. We all need someone we can look up to and go to for guidance. Don't be afraid to approach someone you admire and ask them to be your mentor. In most cases, they will be honored. Most successful people thrive on helping other people because they know, as Zig Ziglar said, "You can have anything you want in life if you will help enough other people get what they want."

I honestly didn't grasp the importance of having a support network until relatively late in my career. I really believed, as so many other people naively believe, that if you work hard and do a good job, then good things will happen for you. While working hard and doing a good job is central and a prerequisite to advancing, once I learned to use the power of networking, *great* things happened for me rapidly. It's not good enough to just *have* a support network; you have to actually *use* your network. You have to take the responsibility and be proactive to seek people out and ask them for help.

Without my support network, I would never have been able to get through my "perfect storm" of life. My network of supporters at work were invaluable to me and helped me think and work through significant career decisions I made – in my case, to take a step back in my career for a while. My support network in my personal life helped save my life. Once I took the initiative and made myself vulnerable by reaching out to them, they were there for me. Whether I just needed them to listen, to allow me to vent, or to just let me cry, they were there.

What I learned most about having a support network and using it is when you ask for help, your supporters will rise to the occasion and do unbelievable things to help you. But the onus is on you to *ask*. No one can help you if they don't know you *want* help or that you need it. So stop right now and think about who your network of supporters are in your work environment and in your personal life. If you can think of at least two in each category, congratulations! Now ask yourself – do you use them? If not, how can you use them? If you couldn't think of at least two network supporters in each category, then you have some work to do. *Get busy!*

8. <u>Make time for yourself.</u>

To any men who may be reading this book – and I hope some are – this principle is especially for the women. Ladies – MAKE TIME FOR

YOUSELF. Men, you can make time for yourselves too! But women especially – we are all so busy with the demands of our lives that we often forget about taking time for us. We are so busy taking care of everyone else and seeing to everyone else's needs that our needs often go neglected or unfulfilled. Part of our female DNA is that we are instinctively nurturers. It's natural for us to be caretakers.

For many years, I did a great job of applying this principle. I actually used to schedule appointments with myself – Me Time, I would call it. Whether it was to get my nails done, have a massage, or just schedule time to read a good trashy novel, it was my time. And I didn't feel guilty about taking the time! I've always been an avid list maker, writing down my list of things to do everyday. I would always include one thing to do for myself for that day. I got great pleasure out of working my list and checking things off. In fact, if I did something and it wasn't on my list, I wrote it on my list just so I could check it off!

In recent years, I violated this principle. In fact, I completely ignored it. I was too busy for me. It was a major mistake. I am a living witness to the fact that you can survive on pure adrenaline for a long period of time, but you will eventually crash and burn. Sooner or later, the mind, body, and soul will merely shut down as if to tell you, "Enough already. Take care of us." At one time, I was so busy trying to keep up with the demands of my work and my life that I was trying to survive on three hours of sleep a night. The human body simply isn't equipped to function on only three hours of sleep night after night. I sacrificed taking care of myself to take care of everybody and everything else.

Speaking of sacrifice – why is it, as women, that many of us have no problem making significant sacrifices for our careers, our families, and even our friends, but when it comes to sacrificing for ourselves, we feel guilty?

It's almost as if we're not worthy. But ladies – we are more than worthy. For any women out there who are trying to have it all – you know better than most – if you break down, lots of things in your life will break down around you. So we simply can't afford to not take care of ourselves because the consequences are significant and ultimately affect everyone in our lives.

Stop and think right now – when is the last time you made time just for you? If it was this week or, better yet, today – EXCELLENT! If it was more than 30 days ago, or worse yet, you can't even remember – then you go get your calendar right now and schedule an appointment with yourself! Making excuses is not allowed. If you think you don't have time, then sacrifice something else for you. You are the most important person in your own life. Without you, you have no life.

9. <u>Celebrate successes and learn from failures</u>.

As we are often busy trying to achieve that next accomplishment, we sometimes forget to take time out to celebrate our successes. Each and every one of us experiences success, no matter how big or small and no matter how significant or insignificant. If we don't take the time to celebrate our successes, it's easy to become disillusioned.

Let me give you an example of what I mean by disillusioned. In the latter part of my career, when I was getting promotions fairly rapidly, I never took time to appreciate or celebrate my accomplishments. Instead, I was constantly thinking about what I could do next. Even though other people viewed me as successful, it didn't feel like success to me. It just felt like I was one step closer to the next big accomplishment. As a result, I had no appreciation for my accomplishments – I didn't celebrate them.

I don't know anyone who has found success without a few failures along the way. The key is to *learn* from your failures so you don't repeat the same mistakes that may have caused you to not to succeed. As Robert F. Kennedy said, "Only those who dare to fail greatly can ever achieve greatly." There is no shame in failing, only in failing to correct our mistakes. As a parent, I feel like I failed on so many levels. But I have learned from those failures, and I will never repeat those mistakes.

Even small milestones should be celebrated. When I started writing this book, I had a target date by which I wanted to have the first five chapters completed. When I reached that milestone on schedule, it was a major accomplishment to me. I celebrated by buying myself five red roses that I put in a beautiful vase on my desk next to my computer. Every time I looked at the roses, it was a reminder to me of my accomplishment. It made me feel great, and it motivated me to reach the next milestone without losing sight of or appreciation for what I had already accomplished.

Give some thought to a recent success you had. Did you do anything to celebrate that success? If so, SPECTACULAR! If not, take the time right now to celebrate, even if it's just by giving yourself a pat on the back or toasting yourself with your favorite beverage. Think about a recent failure you may have experienced. Can you articulate what you learned? If so, WONDERFUL! If not, be careful, as you may make the same mistake again.

One of my favorite quotes regarding success is from the coach Vince Lombardi. He said, "The difference between a successful person and others is not a lack of strength, not a lack of knowledge, but rather a lack of will."

10. <u>Enjoy life. Have fun. Tomorrow isn't promised to you.</u>

This last principle is the most important. We only have one life to live, and we should make the best of all aspects of it. It's okay to have fun! Many of us work extremely hard, and our days are filled with almost every hour being taken. We should ensure that we are *enjoying* ourselves and that we are having fun along the way.

In the aftermath of the 9/11 tragedy, this principle should resonate with most of us more than ever. The people who lost their lives that day didn't start their day with the knowledge that they would not live to see tomorrow. Some of them lost their lives with many fun things they may have *planned* to do but *put off* for another day. This awful catastrophe certainly caused many of us to remember to tell the people we care most about how much we love them. I believe that it fundamentally changed many of our lives, causing us to reevaluate our priorities and what's really important to us in the grand scheme of things.

Many of us have allowed our work to consume our lives, making significant personal sacrifices. But I can assure you that when you leave this world, no matter how important you *think* you are to your work, you *will be replaced*. But you are *irreplaceable* to your family and the people who love you. Whatever you want to do in life, do it now. Tomorrow isn't promised to you.

Always remember, there is only one thing we know for certain when we wake up each morning – that today is the *first* day of the rest of our lives. What we don't know is w*ill it be our last*?

EPILOGUE

A Reclaimed Soul, a New Outlook on Life

When I starting writing this book, I honestly had no idea how it would end. I'm sure I broke every rule of book writing, but I was clearly writing straight from the heart. The story really doesn't end, as this is a journey, and the journey continues. However, now that I've reclaimed my soul from the lost and found, I want to share with you my new outlook on life and the tremendous progress my entire family has made as they have endured this journey with me.

As I write this last chapter, I must say that I have never felt happier and more fulfilled in my entire life. I am healthy in every dimension of my life, physically, emotionally, and spiritually. I feel extremely centered and have so much clarity about who I am and what I want out of life. The façade is gone, and I no longer have a need to pretend that my life is *perfect*. I no longer worry about my image or how other people perceive me, and the only expectations I am trying to live up to are my own – and they are much more realistic than the expectations I had of myself in the past.

I now have true self-acceptance and have learned to love myself, for how can we even begin to love someone else if we don't love ourselves first? My faith in God is stronger than it's ever been. I start and end each day giving him the thanks and the glory that he deserves. For I have come to learn that without him, I am nothing. I am not shy about being a witness for God, sharing the many blessings that he has bestowed upon me. A few years ago, I would have been the last person to openly share my love of God with others. I never thought that I would become a witness and share my personal testimony of the power of prayer and the power of unrelenting faith.

My priorities in my life have changed substantially. I no longer feel the need to live and breathe IBM. In fact, as I write this, my career is somewhat in flux with IBM, and I am uncertain as to what the future holds. But with or without them, I am following my heart and my passion to reach out and help others. I know that however things work out for me, it will be according to God's plan. Dan Pelino recently told me, "When you step out with whatever decision you make, you'll either land on your feet or learn to fly." That was such a profound statement to me, and I'll hold onto that thought forever. I have come to accept that my work is only one aspect of my life – not my entire life or the center of my universe. I have learned to say no more often and don't feel compelled to try to meet everyone else's needs above my own. Family is a top priority for me. I now enjoy being a mother and a wife and no longer feel conflicted about making choices and sacrifices that put them first above my career.

My father continues to cling to life, and I affectionately call him the Energizer Bunny. While he will never see, walk, or talk again and continues to be fed through a tube, he seems comfortable and at peace. His vital signs are actually quite strong, and in November 2003, he celebrated his 80th birthday. It's still very difficult and emotional for me to see him in this stage of life. I have come to accept that when God is ready to call him home, he will. I believe that God has a reason for keeping my father alive. I have many wonderful and magical memories of my father before he became ill, and I hold on to them dearly. One of my fondest memories of him after he became ill but before he stopped talking was when I was visiting him at the nursing home, he sang "You Are My Sunshine" to me. I think of him every day, and I can hear his voice singing that song. I hope my father knows that he is and always will be *my* sunshine.

I remain extremely close to my mother and Granny. Granny is almost 90 now, and I continue to be inspired by her zest for life. While she has slowed down quite a bit and has lost some of her hearing, she still has the energy of a 30-year-old! Several months ago, Granny had the flu, and my mom suggested that she sleep in the bed with her – a king-sized bed – so if Granny needed her in the middle of the night, she could hear her. Well, Granny got better but never moved back to her own room and bed!

I was in Miami visiting recently and crawled into bed between my mom and Granny. It was such a comforting feeling lying next to the two most significant women in my life. The three of us laughed and reminisced, and I felt like I was a kid again. They both fell asleep, but their snoring was a bit much for me. I got out of the bed and watched them sleep for a few moments. I really missed not having my dad there. I felt sad for my mom, as I knew how much she missed him. She had spent over 50 years with her soul mate, and now instead of the warmth of his body at night, it was her mother who was in bed with her. I thought about the fact that my mom was just a kid herself when she and my dad married. I was so proud of my mom – a woman who had beat incredible odds. I knew that I was so much like my mom – more than I wanted to admit. I had her strength and her courage, and I now had learned to have her tremendous faith in God.

I left my mom's room and actually went into Granny's room to sleep instead of what used to be my own room. As I was lying in Granny's bed, I had that same safe feeling I used to feel as a child when I used to sleep with her. I wondered how many more years Granny would be around. I pulled the covers close to my face and felt comforted by the smell of her sheets. I slept like a baby that night. The next morning, I woke up to the smell of bacon and eggs. I went into the kitchen and there was Granny, cooking me breakfast as she had done when I was a kid. I said, "Granny, you do too much. I should be cooking you breakfast." She said, "Child, this is what keeps me young," as she proceeded to bundle up the garbage to take it out. I chuckled and was amazed that at almost 90 years old, she was still my same old Granny, who could do no wrong in my eyes.

My mom now walks with the aid of a walker, as she has some back problems that keep her in constant pain. But even in the midst of her chronic pain, she keeps going and continues to have a positive outlook on life. My mom is an incredible woman, and while I have always loved her deeply, in the past few years I have come to truly appreciate her and everything she taught me growing up. I know she still worries about me continuously. I no longer tell her not to worry, as I now well know, "A good mother never stops worrying about her children."

My sisters, Berthina and Annette, continue to be a great source of strength for me. They pray for me and with me often. They were instrumental in helping me to come through and survive the storm. Annette still makes me laugh hysterically, and Berthina is still very protective of me. I have an immense appreciation for their unconditional love, support, and guidance. I am so thankful to have them in my life. My brother, Lorenzo, and I have grown closer and talk a little more frequently these days. Even though our conversations are generally brief, he never fails to tell me how much he loves me and how proud he is of me.

I used to think that I really didn't have many real friends. But I was blessed to find that I have an abundance of true friends, male and female, who love me and care for me just as I am. I have come to appreciate them and value their friendship more than ever and am not shy about calling on them when I need help. They may never know how instrumental they were to me in my journey to reclaim my soul.

My marriage is on solid ground. After Jim and I were briefly separated, he returned home and we reconciled. We were not ready to throw in the towel and give up. We took our wedding vows seriously – for richer or poorer, in sickness and in health, till death do us part. We decided that divorce simply was not an option; it was a copout. We owed it to ourselves and our children to do whatever work was necessary together and individually to put the pieces of our marriage back together. It was like falling in love all over again. We have both learned to accept each other just as we are – with all of our flaws and all of our little idiosyncrasies. We learned how to handle conflict and differences in a healthier and more productive way. We both let go of the anger, resentment, and hurt that had built up over the years. We learned the power of forgiveness and that moving forward meant not looking back and dwelling on the past. Neither of us could change any of the events that happened yesterday. We learned from our mistakes and moved on.

I am madly in love with Jim and still get butterflies in my stomach when our eyes meet in a passing glance or when he touches me in a way that tells me, "I love you." He knows me so well and can read me like a book. In fact, he has been one of my greatest supporters through the process of writing this book. He listened to chapter after chapter late at night as I would read to him in bed even though I knew he was tired. He encouraged me to keep my dream alive and listened to my ideas and gave me valuable and honest feedback. In watching me go through my journey of making changes in my life, he too was inspired to make some changes of his own. He has always had a love and passion for music. He got serious about his music and has become an even more gifted and talented pianist than he already was. Sometimes, I sit in my home office and listen to his piano playing, and the beauty of his music brings tears to my eyes. Our marriage still isn't perfect – as no marriage is. But we truly love each other unconditionally, and our marriage is stronger than it's ever been.

Recently, I was on the train one evening on my way to New York City. A young gentleman sat next to me, and I smiled at him, acknowledging his presence. We began to engage in small talk. He commented, "You have the most beautiful smile I've ever seen. You look like a very happy person. I can feel your energy."

I wasn't really sure if he was sincere in his comment or if this was just some creative come-on, but I said, "Thank you."

He then asked, "Are you married?"

"Yes, I am."

"Are you happily married?"

I paused before I responded and then looked him directly in the eyes and said, "I'm very happily married, more than you can imagine."

He responded, "Wow, I've never heard a person respond with so much passion and conviction. Congratulations. I haven't met too many people who are truly happily married."

We sat in silence for the rest of the train ride, as we both took out books to read. I couldn't help but think how blessed I was that I had my soul back. I really *was* happy – more than this young man could have ever known.

I didn't talk a lot about my younger daughter, Jennifer, in this book, but the thought of her is what saved my life. She was my silent strength as I went through my journey of reclaiming my soul. She is now 14 and has blossomed into an amazing young lady. She continues to do great in school and is very confident and comfortable with herself. She is a master at not letting other people influence her decisions and has handled normal adolescent peer pressure remarkably well. She is a talented artist and a talented writer as well. She still prefers to be alone, although she does enjoy talking on the phone and via instant messenger on the Internet with her friends. She has yet to attend a school dance, as she finds them boring. Getting her to go to the mall is like torturing her. She is not your typical 14-year-old girl. She is not materialistic at all and rarely asks for anything other than the occasional video game. She is very caring and giving. She has a genuine regard for other people's feelings. She gets upset when she hears anyone say something negative about another person. She truly tries to see the good in everyone.

It's ironic to me that Jennifer, the one I complained so much about when she was an infant, ended up being my greatest comforter in my time of despair. She has a level of emotional maturity well beyond her years. She always knows just the right thing to say to me. She instinctively knows when I just need a hug from her, even though her nature is not that of a very touchy-feely person. We have developed an extremely close bond that I can't explain. I look at her and it's as if I'm looking in the mirror at myself when I was her age. We look almost identical, and she actually gets a little tired of hearing everyone tell her so. Jennifer's love significantly helped me get through the storm. The thought that I almost left her and that she would have been the one to find me slumped over the steering wheel of my car is incomprehensible to me now and sends chills up my spine.

This story was as much about my oldest, Kristin's life as it was about mine. I am happy to report that she is doing well and has come a long way in her own personal journey. She is now almost 16 and attends a four-year college prep boarding school in Connecticut, only 40 minutes from our home. She loves it there and is making great progress. I feel like I've got my daughter back, as she is not the same disturbed teenager that she was when I sent her away in September of 2002. She has endured her own process of self-discovery, and I think that she now enjoys a measure of true self-acceptance.

She stills struggles at times with making good choices, but she has learned that she is totally accountable for her actions and has to suffer the consequences of her own choices. She has learned that Jim and I love her *unconditionally* and that our only expectations of her are that she does the best that she can do – whatever that is. She now understands that we accept her just as she is and have no preconceived notions of who she will or will not be.

She has a love of photography and enjoys writing poetry. During her 112 days in the wilderness, she filled up more than 20 journals, and she hopes to someday write her own story about her experiences, targeted toward teenagers. She too has blossomed into a beautiful young lady inwardly and outwardly. She has a tremendous sense of humor and a smile that can light up a dim room. She is learning to use the abundance of energy that she has in positive ways. Her school requires students to volunteer for community-service projects, and she takes great pleasure in volunteering at a preschool working with children – many of whom have attention deficit disorder (ADD).

Kristin and Jennifer have become much closer to each other, and it's like music to my ears to hear their chatter and laughter when Kristin is home for school breaks. Kristin is very proud of her younger sister and enjoys bragging about her artistic abilities to her friends. She reinforces to Jennifer to never make the mistakes that she made. She is very protective of her and loves to give her advice about boys.

Kristin and I both now understand that, for a long time, it was as if she was in the ocean drowning, and I was in there with her trying to save her. If you've ever tried to save a drowning person's life, then you understand that the drowning victim will push the rescuer down under the water as they're trying to save themselves. I know this well from my own childhood neardrowning incident. Many people have drowned while trying to rescue someone else. That's exactly what happened to me – I was trying to save Kristin, but she was drowning me. We now both understand that I can only throw her a life ring, and it's up to her to grab hold of it and start pulling herself in. I have thrown her countless life rings through the course of this treacherous journey we've both been on. She has finally grabbed hold of them and is pulling herself in, getting closer and closer to the shore each and every day.

I now live by my 10 guiding principles and am taking great care not to stray from them. I am very proud of myself and how far I've come over the last 18 months.

It's the end of 2003, and Jim, Kristin, Jennifer, and I shared a very special and intimate Christmas with just the four of us. We had so much to celebrate and be thankful for. It was so nice to have all us together as a family again and to see the spark in each of our eyes. As I sat sleepy eyed while we opened our presents, I caught the reflections of Jim, Kristin, and Jennifer in the ornaments on the tree. It was a magical moment for me as I realized that my three greatest gifts were sitting before my very eyes.

I am excited about the New Year, 2004. The past year, my soul was so lost in the deep dungeons of the lost and found, but I can stand tall now and shout to the world, "**I've reclaimed my soul from the lost and found,** and I don't plan to ever let it end up there again!"

WANT TO SHARE YOUR STORY?

If you've reclaimed your own soul from the lost and found, you're invited to submit your story to be considered for Lisa's next book, which will be a collection of inspirational accounts from people who have overcome insurmountable obstacles and reclaimed their souls from the lost and found. Whether you've experienced a true miracle or have found genuine peace and accord in your life, other people can learn from and be inspired by your experiences. Everyone has a story to tell, so why not share yours with the world?

Stories should not exceed 2000 words and must be uplifting, inspirational, or educational. Please submit only original work. You will be credited for your work if it is selected for publication.

Please send your submission via e-mail to lwhaley@lifeworksynergy.com. You also can mail or fax your submission to:

Life Work Synergy, LLC
Suite 331
9 Brush Hill Road
New Fairfield, CT 06812
Fax: 203-746-3495

Be sure to include all contact information, including your name, phone number, mailing address, and e-mail address.

If you would like to contact Lisa regarding speaking engagements, workshops, or coaching services, please e-mail her at lwhaley@lifeworksynergy.com

ABOUT THE AUTHOR

Lisa J. Whaley is the Founder and President of Life Work Synergy, an organization dedicated to helping women and men find realistic solutions to achieving synergy and harmony between their personal and professional lives. She uses personal experiences she encountered managing her life as an executive with IBM while raising a family, to motivate clients and teach them how to apply disciplined practices to their hectic lives. She is a frequent motivational speaker and is a member of The International Coach Federation. Ms. Whaley mentors young women and men at risk. She holds a Bachelor of Science degree in Business Management from Hampton University and resides in New Fairfield, Connecticut, with her husband, Jim, and their two daughters.

Printed in the United States
24539LVS00001B/222

9 781414 072319